# -TALL TALES-

## SHORT STORIES
## FROM A LONG
## GAME WARDEN CAREER

## WASHINGTON FISH &
## WILDLIFE
## OFFICER STEVE ROGERS
## (RETIRED)

Printed by:  **Create Space**
Distributed by: www.amazon.com



ISBN- 979-8-7200-98940

Cover created by- **Bruce Weild, www.b-creative.ca/design**

# DEDICATION

This book is dedicated to my wonderful wife, Cindy, who put up with my long hours and many distractions over the years.

"The real wealth of the Nation lies in the resources of the earth - soil, water, forests, minerals, and wildlife."

## -RACHEL CARSON-

# Chapter 1 - "It Takes a Sense of Humor"

After working 33 years as a Game Warden in Washington State I retired to live the dream in Upper Kittitas County. Now, after being retired for 9 years I was asked by a local newspaper writer-friend to relate a story or two for the public to read, maybe something funny (I know, most people in law enforcement usually don't have friends in the news media, but…). Hmm. Well, I often found that what may be funny to me wasn't very funny to the people I was in contact with on the job. They didn't always "get" my sense of humor. This all got me to thinking I should jot down a few ideas. Like these below:

I was up in the Alpine Lakes Wilderness working the "High Hunt" with my neighboring Officer, Gary, back in about '91. This early buck deer season started on September 15th. It was a 25-mile trip in the truck pulling a loaded horse trailer up a horrible logging road. We packed in 9 miles on horses and a pack mule to Michael Lake and set up a great wall tent camp just above the lake. It was a popular deer hunting area and we had seen several camps on the way in. We were working "under cover", dressed as regular hunters. The weather was good, and we looked forward to several days in the High Country.

The nice thing about a pack mule is being able to bring some of the comforts along, such as lawn chairs, steaks, wall tent, etc.

The evening before the opener Gary and I were sitting by the campfire fixing to have a thick steak, a green salad with ranch dressing, and a sip or two of anti-freeze - it was a little chilly up there at 8,000 feet. We sat in our lawn chairs and watched several deer on one hillside and two mountain goats on another. It was a perfectly clear evening but starting to get cold.

I thought I would try calling Dispatch on the radio to see if they could hear me. Having a radio signal that far back in the hills was iffy at best. I had no answer from them, but a Fish & Wildlife Biologist came on the air and asked where we were. I told him and he said he was camped in a different area over on the west side of the mountains. We were pretty sure this guy had hiked in with a backpack. Gary, with his usual twinkle in the eye, said to ask him what he was having for dinner. You see, Gary is a bit of a smart-aleck and practical joker.

Well, this poor guy answered, "You know, the usual freeze-dried stuff". Gary giggled and said to tell him what we were having. Trying not to chuckle I told the guy about the steaks, salad and cocktails. Never heard another word from the poor guy. No sense of humor! I hoped he made it through the high hunt okay.

You know how those granola crunchers are - probably didn't even have a campfire.

At daylight the next morning we were up and hiking down the trail to see if we could find any hunting activity. We got to a point where we could see a big hillside on Moonlight Basin, with good cover. Sure enough, we heard a shot very nearby and saw a guy in hunter orange sneaking along the hill into some thick brush. We kept losing sight of him. Then, there was a second shot, probably to finish off the buck. Suddenly, we saw the hunter come out of the brush, rifle slung on his shoulder, and headed down the hill to the main trail. It didn't appear he had time to notch his tag and we thought, being the suspicious guys that we were, he probably killed a small, illegal deer. They had to have at least 3 antler points on one side to be legal. It was one of those "good bet" moments. We both had many years of experience on the job and were pretty sure this was one of those moments.

Gary and I were working undercover in civilian clothes to look like hunters. We hustled down the trail and met this guy as he reached the main trail. We asked if he got a buck and he said, "Yeah". He wouldn't make eye contact with us, another "indicator". I asked if he needed some help getting it down to camp. He just said, "Nope, I'll get my buddy to help". Gary says, "We'd be glad to help - let's go back up and get it". The guy said "no". Then Gary showed him his badge and said "yes". And that was that. We found the deer to be a small 2- point and not tagged as required. We felt he would have left it there to rot if we had not witnessed this.

We had the guy retrieve the deer, field dress it so it would not go to waste and told him he must haul it down to the Forest Service to be turned over to the food bank. He did so and paid his fine. Case closed. I will note that he was very unhappy with us butting into his hunt. He was not laughing about it.

When we left the area, we were riding down the trail and met some backpackers. I warned them to get way up off the trail because "this mule likes to kick". You should have seen them scramble up the hill. As we pulled along-side of them I asked if they had any that gorp stuff. I said the mule loves gorp and it would be nice if they gave him some. They wouldn't get anywhere near that darned kickin' mule. Just no sense of humor.

A couple years later I was back in the Michael Lake area to work the high hunt, this time in uniform. I rode into a camp to check the hunters. Here was this same fella that shot the 2-point and I said, "Howdy, remember me"?  I smiled and thought I was being polite and friendly. He just glared at me and turned away. Hmmm, just no sense of humor A-tall.

# Chapter 2 - "Bucky"

Often times Game Wardens have a few tricks up their sleeves in order to catch poachers. A poacher is someone who kills wildlife illegally. Most of us agree that "routine patrol" is pretty unproductive time since being in the right place at the right time is difficult in a large patrol area. Being there, then, is pure luck when you actually find a violation in progress.

One of our tricks was called "Bucky" the robo-deer. He was built on a lightweight frame with a small battery-operated motor that turned the head and "wagged" the tail. It had a remote operating system that could be used from another, nearby location, out of the line of fire.

One night during archery deer season three of us took Bucky up to a ridge along a Forest Service road where hunters would be coming out from hunting. We placed "Bucky" 20 feet off the road against a small hill with brush. It was on a curve where vehicle headlights would catch the "eyes" on the decoy. Using artificial light to aid in hunting big game is illegal as it gives the "hunter" an unfair advantage by making the deer stop, blinded by the bright lite.

Along about midnight a vehicle came slowly down the road. Two of us were in the brush across from Bucky, while our other partner was down the road in the "chase" vehicle. We watched as the vehicle neared the decoy. The headlights lit up the eyes and the car stopped. The passenger door opened, and a man stepped out with a bow.

I called the chase car on the radio and told him to be ready, "we have a live one". We could see enough in the headlight glow to know the passenger was knocking an arrow. Then we heard a "thud" as the arrow hit the decoy. Apparently, the guy didn't hear, or didn't register the thud, and he knocked another arrow and shot. Just as he was about to use a third arrow my partner and I walked up behind him and announced, "Game Warden, you're under arrest!" The guy was so focused on the deer, which for some reason had still not moved, that he didn't understand who was talking to him. It was surreal to hear unknown voices from out of the night in the middle of the woods.

After all was said and done, we had seized the bow and written tickets for hunting big game after legal hours, hunting with aid of artificial light and shooting from a public roadway. The driver was cited for complicity on the same charges. Both were totally ashamed of themselves.

Another chance came before light on opening morning of archery deer season above town on logging roads. It was the same scenario with the decoy on a curve and two of us hiding in the brush. At 45 minutes before legal shooting time a small truck came up the road, went past the decoy, stopped and backed up to shine the headlights on the "deer". Tom and I could hear the two occupants talking and trying to decide if they should try it. I heard the driver tell his friend to go for it. It appeared that the 3 by 4 antlered buck was legal, except for the time of day. The passenger got out and shot an arrow at "Bucky" and hit it. I heard him say, "oh, s**t". We were just a few feet behind him, and we told him, "Freeze, Game Warden". That about scared the pee-waddin' out of him.

As we were filling out the tickets, I asked both men what their occupation was, as it was a blank on the citation form that was required to be filled in. One of them mumbled something I couldn't hear, and I asked to repeat that. He said, "We are both attorneys". It was just starting to get light enough to see and Tom's eyes met mine, both of us smiling. We charged them with hunting big game during the closed season and they both paid their fines without argument.

One early morning before light on opening day of muzzleloader cow and spike bull elk season we had set up a cow elk decoy on a main road leading up into a popular elk hunting area north of Ellensburg. The ground was very hard and we couldn't find a good place to stand the decoy so we just sorta leaned it against a fence post. It looked kinda funky, but we saw headlights coming and decided to see what would happen.

The first vehicle up the road saw the eyes in the headlights and pulled over on a wide spot on the road. Several other rigs were coming up behind him and he waved his arm out the window, flagging them by as if to say, "This one's mine guys, keep going".

It was still pitch-black dark out when we saw a long barrel stick out the window and shoot the elk. The elk did not move. Elk never just stand still when a gun goes off. I don't know what he was thinking but he must have been pretty focused on getting "his" elk. He got out and started to reload his single shot black powder rifle. Again, he thought he was all alone in the world and didn't understand who was yelling at him from the darkness. When he finally figured out the problem, he was surrounded by four Game Wardens. His first comment was. "I would never do something like this!!" Well, he just did, and he was cited for the usual charges plus having a loaded rifle in a motor vehicle and hunting with the aid of a motor vehicle. He paid his fines without argument and lost his hunting privilege for two years.

I think the next decoy we might make is a grouse to put alongside the road - might be kinda fun. Who could pass that up? I used to show the photo of the elk decoy, tied to a tree, to all the hunters who asked me where I "have 'em all tied up"?

# Chapter 3 - "You need a fishing license here?"

**Thorp Lake**

In all 50 States a fishing license is required to fish for game fish. This includes trout, even wild trout in the wilderness. I had decided it was time to check for fishing activity in the high country of Kittitas County, Washington and planned a three-day loop on horseback.

After hauling the horses 25 miles from Cle Elum to Fish (Tucquala) Lake, I rode up past Squaw Lake to Cathedral Rock, across the ridge and down to Deep Lake. My, what a view from the ridgetop. The weather was perfect and, being Friday, I figured there would be hikers everywhere. But it was very quiet, and I found nobody fishing. I spent the night below Deep Lake at Spinola Creek meadows. The next day I hiked up to Deer and Vicenti Lakes. There was no one around. One of the perks of the job is that I needed to "sample" the fishing at these lakes and report numbers and sizes of fish to the Fish Bug (that's what we called the biologists) in Yakima. I even had a report form to fill out to document the fish. And they pay me to do this.

It was a perfect day with sunshine, clear skies, and about 70 degrees. Surrounded by high mountains Vicenti Lake was a clear and beautiful sight to behold. I pulled out my break-down fly rod and went at it. I caught what looked like Cutthroat/Golden Trout Hybrids. They were nice 12-to-14-inch fish and they were biting everything I threw at them. And, by the way, I did have my fishing license with me. For once in my life, I actually got tired of casting and retrieving fish.

By mid-day I was back to the horses and headed down Spinola Creek to Waptus Lake. Waptus is a very popular destination for hikers and horse riders and there are lots of camping sites. Riding down along the lake I managed to locate several people actively fishing. They weren't catching many fish but were having a great "wilderness experience". Everyone I checked had a valid fishing license. And they were happy to see me out checking.

I set up camp at the old Forest Service campsite back off the main trail along Spinola Creek. Before dinner I decided to ride around to the Quick Creek campsite and see if anyone was there. As I rode in, I saw a man fishing at the edge of the lake. I was wearing my uniform and I greeted him with, "How's it going, catching anything"? He looked around at me, had a sudden realization, and his eyes went down toward his feet. Oh, oh.

I got down and tied my horse up. Again, I asked the guy if he had any luck. He said he had caught nothing and wasn't "really" fishing. I told him it kinda looked to me like he was fishing and asked to see his license. He looked up at me and said, "You mean I need a fishing license way back here in the wilderness"? He said he thought this was like a national park where you don't need a license. I explained the bad news and told him that you even need a license in national parks, even if they are free.

I issued a citation for fishing without a valid license and told him to cease fishing. I rode back to camp and had a nice steak dinner and slept like a baby.

The next day, Sunday, I rode back up along the lake and found no other people fishing. Back at Deep Lake I saw some people on the far side of the lake and one guy was fishing. I got my fly rod out and did some "sampling" for the Bugs while I watched the fisherman across the lake. There were two women with him who were not fishing. After a while I saddled up and rode around the lake to contact them. As I rode in the guy put his fishing pole down and greeted me with a big smile. He said, "I'm a Deputy Sheriff and I always wondered if you guys ever checked this area - great to see you here".

We shook hands and I introduced myself, stating that I do indeed check this area often. I asked to see his fishing license. He said, "You mean I need a license here in the wilderness"? I explained that most of the fish in the high lakes have been planted by the Department of Fish and Wildlife, that it costs money to do so, and that license fees go to pay for that. And "yes, you need to buy a license".

His next comment was a surprise. He said, "aw, come on, can't you give a "Brother Officer" a break"? I said, "Since you put it that way, NO"! and told him I'd probably write my own Mother up in the same situation. I wrote the ticket and had him sign it, with the warning that he must contact the Cle Elum District Court within 2 weeks and take care of this or the court will issue an arrest warrant. He didn't like that and became kind of indignant. I told him I was sorry he felt that way, got on my horse and rode out. Of all the nerve! I could still remember the good old days when, if caught in violation of the rules, most people would accept it, say, "You got me", and shake my hand. Not this guy - guess he thought he was above the law.

**From Ivanhoe Lake looking down at Waptus Lake**

The Washington Department of Fish and Wildlife and the Chelan County PUD used to plant rainbow trout in the upper Wenatchee River. It was a huge draw for people from all over the state. There was a lot of crime involved with this resource including over-limits of fish. At the time the daily trout limit in rivers was 8 fish over 8 inches long. Some people just can't help taking more than their fair share - that's where the Game Wardens come in.

The Officer assigned to this area was Gary Jones, a no-nonsense Warden with 30 years on and a very good sense of humor. It was always a pleasure to work with him as he seemed to attract "business" and had so much fun doing his job.

One season Gary called for an emphasis patrol on the river due to many reports of violations. He organized eight of us for a two-day emphasis on over-limits. Some guys would be in uniform and the rest under cover.

Gary and I hooked up to work together. In civies, with fishing gear and a cooler, we waded across the river to a sand bar where we could watch a big crowd of people fishing on the highway side of the river. The plan was to pretend to fish, watch for violations, and call them in to the uniformed guys.

We kept a notebook handy and wrote down the time and description when we saw someone catch a fish. We named everyone by their clothing or appearance, such as "red hat guy, green shirt girl, little fat boy, etc." so the uniforms could find them.

We watched a guy in a red jacket catch his limit of trout, go up to his truck, and come back without the jacket and wearing a different colored hat. This was obviously an intentional act as he started fishing again. As soon as he caught another trout we called in and described the violator to the uniforms. These people had no idea we were over there watching them and probably wondered how they got caught.  Gary said, "Listen to this". He got on the radio to the guys in uniform and said, "The chopper's running low on fuel - heading to town, back in 20 minutes". It was so hilarious to watch everyone standing near the officer's portable radio start looking up in the air for that darned chopper.

# Chapter 4 - "Dummies"

It was always very satisfying to actually catch someone intentionally breaking law. There will always be someone out there who can't seem to obey the rules governing hunting and fishing. Whether it is greed or just plain disdain for rules in general, there will always be a need for fish and wildlife law enforcement.

Sometimes, though, normally law-abiding people just make mistakes. It may be due to misreading the regulations, which can be intimidating at times, or not understanding the rules due to language barriers or being from different cultures.

State Patrol Dispatched called me one Sunday morning and told me that two troopers were out with two men and two dead cow elk on private property just outside of town. The weather was cold and there were several inches of fresh snow on the ground. As I pulled up to the scene, I could see blood everywhere on the snow - it was a pretty gory looking sight. My first thought was that these guys had no idea what they were doing.

I talked with the Troopers and got the ID's and hunting licenses from the two suspects. It seems they had cow elk permits for an area on the Quilomene Wildlife Area some 60 miles to the East of here.

I introduced myself to the two men and explained that they were on posted private property and a long way from where they should be. The landowner had reported them, and he was pretty upset as he does not allow hunting on his land. I told them they were in violation and advised them of their rights under Miranda.

**Trooper James with two illegal cow elk**

They agreed to talk to me and were very sorry. They were covered in blood and were not wearing normal hunting clothing. They said they were from a church congregation in Seattle, were not experienced hunters, had never field dressed anything before, and had applied for the permits to try to get meat to share with their group. They tried to follow a map and directions but had never been east of the mountains before and had no idea where they were.

I thought, "Oh, boy!". This was one of those situations that would require some extra thought rather than just throwing the book at them. These two guys were what we in the Game Enforcement business called "Dummies". They had no clue what they were doing and definitely should not have been out there doing what they were doing.

At that time, we were taking confiscated deer and elk to the Kittitas County Jail to feed prisoners. I asked the Troopers to call the jail and see if they had some Trustees that could come up and get the meat. I issued a single citation to each for hunting in a closed area and seized their rifles for evidence. I also took their pictures to show they were all covered in blood.

I explained that I would try to smooth things with the landowner and hope they would not be charged with trespassing and go to jail. Further, I explained that there were a host of other charges I could hit them with but, that I didn't think they were poachers and hoped they learned their lesson from this. They assured me that they would never hunt again.

Another year, on opening day of mule deer season, I had a call from the patrolman for the Boise Cascade Timber Company in the Teanaway River Valley. He said he was patrolling behind closed gates and found a group of guys with a 6-point bull elk down. They were in the process of dragging it out whole to their vehicle about a half mile away. He said they were all grinning and saying, "Big Deer". He told them to stop and wait for the game warden. None of them spoke good English.

When I arrived, I saw the huge rack on the bull and thought, Oh, Boy, here we go again". I contacted the suspects and asked for their hunting licenses and deer tags, which they all produced, all valid. I determined which of the six had shot the elk and tried to explain the difference between an elk and deer. Using the hunting regulations pamphlet, I showed them pictures and finally got through to them.

Other than shooting the wrong animal they had done everything right - licenses/tags, walked in on the road, notched the tag, etc.

I had them load the elk into my patrol truck. I issued a citation to the shooter for possessing a closed season elk and did my best to explain what he had to do. I took his rifle as evidence. I couldn't call these guys "dummies" but they sure had no idea what they did wrong. They were very respectful and, I think, glad they weren't going to jail.

# Chapter 5 - "Poachers, not dummies"

One year in late spring I had received a call from a County road crew working along Lake Cle Elum. A flagger had noticed a small Toyota pickup full of men going up the road for a couple of days in a row and thought they looked suspicious. On the third day the flagger called Dispatch to say she saw a rifle in the vehicle with 5 males. It was 10 am on a warm, sunny morning. I contacted the flagger who said the Toyota went on up the road but did not know where they went above the construction site. There were numerous possibilities.

I asked Dispatch if there were any County Deputies in the area that could come up to help me. A Kittitas County Deputy arrived within a half hour and we made a plan. I had him patrol along the main road while I checked spur roads.

I got about a mile up the French Cabin Creek Road when I saw a blue Toyota pickup coming toward me. I radioed the Deputy where I was and stopped the pickup. I was surprised that the driver spoke good English and I asked if they were hunting. He said, "no hunting, just drive 'round". There were three in the front seat and two in back, one holding an AK47 rifle. The truck had a canopy cover on the back.

The Deputy arrived at that moment. We had the men get out of the vehicle and I secured the rifle, which was loaded. On the floor of the back seat, I found a .22 rifle and a 12-gauge shotgun, also loaded. All five of the men sat on the side of the road with their hands on their heads as if they had been here before.

My Sergeant came on the radio and asked if I was ok. I asked him to come up and join us. Then I saw the blood on the back bumper. I asked the driver if they had shot an animal. He said, "No", and none of the others spoke a word.

I looked in the back window of the canopy. There was a 50-gallon trash can inside, a blue tarp sticking out of the can, and I saw a deer leg sticking out from under the tarp.

I started collecting IDs from the suspects, all from the Seattle area. When my Sergeant arrived, I explained everything, including the deer leg. He said that looks like evidence of a crime in plain view. We opened the back of the truck and pulled out a doe deer from the trash can. The deer had been shot and was very freshly killed.

We did a quick necropsy, found it had been shot in the neck, and saw that it was a pregnant doe, probably just weeks from giving birth.

I issued citations to all 5 suspects for possession of two deer in the closed season and possession of 3 loaded firearms in a motor vehicle. I seized the deer and guns, and we released the suspects. None of them ever came to court and, to this day many years later, they still have warrants for their arrest. This was a good example of knowingly poaching.

As the 1997 early archery deer season was underway, I received a call via cell phone from a hunter. He had hiked a mile into his tree stand before light and was hoping to see a big buck that had been on his trail camera. As it started to get light, he heard a vehicle coming up a nearby logging road. The vehicle, a black SUV, was driving very slowly as if hunting. It arrived at a landing, and the end of the road, and the doors opened. The witness was almost a mile away from that landing. Then he heard a rifle shot.

He saw the passenger running up a hill and heard another shot. The witness was beyond mad! He lowered his gear and climbed down from the tree stand. He hiked down to his vehicle and drove out to the Last Resort to find cellular service.  The dispatcher patched him through to my phone and I got the story. The road was quite a ways up in the hills above Lake Cle Elum.

I told dispatch what was happening and the location. There was a state trooper not far away and he offered to come back me up. That started a chain of events leading to my patrol truck and a string of 5 WA State Patrol vehicles in a line going up a rough logging road. It would have made a great picture.

I knew the exact location of the landing and, upon arriving in the area, could see the SUV parked. I pulled up behind it and got out just as two men came up over the top of the hill ahead. One trooper and I met them and asked what they were doing. They said they were just out riding around and got out to look over the hills.

Now these two looked like your typical, everyday dirt-bags with dirty clothes, long hair, tattoos and earrings - Yes, I was profiling. Sorry! And they had just lied to me.

We knew they were lying, and I went ahead and asked what they did with the deer they shot. They denied anything about a deer and said they don't have any guns. I told them they were seen with a rifle and that they had shot twice. I said that the Troopers have a way to test for gunshot residue and, that they had best come clean now. One guy said I was "full of shit" and that they were leaving. I told them they weren't going anywhere until I got the straight scoop from them.

The Troopers took the two down to the vehicles while I took off up the hill and looked down the backside. It took me a few minutes, but I finally found a dead buck deer with huge antlers. It was partially covered with brush. There was no tag on it and it had not been gutted.

Back at the vehicles the two denied having a rifle and knew nothing of the dead deer. I told them I would find the rifle and then they would be charged with obstructing an Officer along with everything else. No response.

Two troopers and I spread out on the hillside where we had first seen the suspects. After looking for about ten minutes one of the Troops found a scoped .30-06 rifle stashed under a log. It was still loaded. Searching around the parking area by the suspect's vehicle we found a fresh spent .30-06 shell casing.

One of these troopers was a detective and he had all of his investigative equipment in his car. This included electronic recording gear and more. He suggested we split the two up, "Mirandize" them, and see if he can get a statement from them.

Long story short, these two Knuckleheads decided their goose was cooked and decided to come clean. Their statements were recorded and later transcribed by the State Patrol Detachment Office Manager. One of the guys said his father is a Sergeant in a Westside County and said, "my dad is probably gonna kill me".

The deer was saved for the food bank, rifle seized for forfeiture, and the two dudes were issued mandatory court summonses. The witness received a nice reward of 10 preference points towards a permit drawing. I wrote a nice letter of thanks to the State Patrol for their fine help. The bad guys received a hefty fine, paid $2000 in restitution for the trophy buck, and lost hunting privileges for a couple years. This was a great example of cooperative, cross-agency assistance. I may not have made that case without the troopers. I think they were mostly happy to get off the I-90 corridor and writing speeding tickets.

**Mule Deer at the Rachel Lake Trailhead**

# Chapter 6 - "Nuisance Wildlife"

Nationwide, Game Wardens are called to do a lot of things beside enforce the game laws. Some of those other duties fall under the heading of "nuisance wildlife". Calls for service in this category can include such things as injured birds, beavers damming creeks and causing flooding, hawks killing chickens, cougars killing goats, and herding elk out of hay barns.

When I was hired, I became what used to be called a Control Agent (wildlife damage control) in the greater Tacoma/Pierce County area of Western Washington, handling hundreds of calls on raccoons, porcupines, and beaver. During the six years I was in Tacoma I live trapped and relocated approximately 6000 raccoons. Most were ear-tagged, and the tag numbers logged in a journal. When I started re-catching raccoons that had travelled back to Tacoma from the south end of the county, I decided it was time to stop the relocation program and just euthanize them. They certainly were not endangered and most of them carried dangerous roundworms and other pests/diseases. Most of the time these animals were caught in the summer and their fur was not worth anything.

My training supervisor, Bob, taught me a lot about trapping beaver and blowing beaver dams. Also, I got to be good friends with a trapper from Buckley named Dick Streepy. Dick took me with him on several jaunts to the beaver swamps to teach me. He used a lure made from the castor glands and the small oil sac next to the gland. He called his mixture" stink-um-up-Joe" and it really did attract the beaver. We removed a lot of beaver causing problems with dams and I learned how to skin and put up the pelts for sale. Another Trapper named George Sovie taught me the finer points of live-trapping raccoons. The best bait was large, white marshmallows. When I left the area six years later George became the go to guy as a licensed nuisance wildlife control raccoon expert. I think he got rich doing it and was busy at it until he died many years later.

Speaking of blowing beaver dams, another "rookie" and I got to go along with Bob to see how to use a two-part liquid/powder explosive to remove a beaver dam in a culvert on a logging road. The resultant backup of water was threatening to wash out the road and log trucks needed to use it, NOW!

The other "rookie", Mike, and I were hired together, and we were all eyes and ears hoping to learn as much as possible from this more experienced supervisor. We called ourselves "The Bold New Breed" and we were going to be the best there ever was.

Well, ol' Bob showed us how to mix the explosive, use detonation cord and caps, how to safely attach the caps, and finally place the explosive into the culvert plug in such a way that it would blow the plug out but not damage the metal culvert. Sounds good, right?

When all was set, we ran a wire to a safe location, attached it to the battery, and pushed the plunger. I have no idea what went wrong but nothing happened. Now our supervisor had explained all the safety aspects including what to do and how long to wait in case the darned thing didn't blow. He said you have to wait an hour just in case it has a delayed reaction. Bob wasn't having any of that. I had been in the Navy for four years, but I had never heard some of the words coming out of his mouth. He went storming up to the culvert and started checking connections. He was so mad that he even mixed up a couple more sticks of explosive, just to make sure this time!!

I guess we were learning quite a lesson that day. When the plunger went down this time the charge went off. It was very loud and sprayed rocks and mud a long way, all the way to where we were hiding. When the smoke cleared the beaver dam was gone along with most of the culvert. The air turned blue again and we rookies were looking for a new place to hide. From Bob. I have no idea what he told the loggers about the road damage but at least the water was flowing again.

I could write a whole book just on my experiences with "problem" wildlife, good, bad, and hilarious. Like the time I was trying to remove a litter of baby 'coons from the attic of an elderly couple and got attacked by mama 'coon. The poor old folks downstairs heard my yelling and screaming but were totally helpless. I finally had to whack Mama on the head with my flashlight to get her to let go of my hand.

And the time I was hauling a bunch of young raccoons in a cage to a new location for release. Somehow, they got the latch open, crawled into the truck bed, and one crawled up to my open window - all while driving down I-5 at 60 mph. I quickly rolled up the window but got the baby 'coon caught by the neck as I was trying to pull to the shoulder. I rolled the window back down and the thing jumped inside the cab. Luckily this little guy was docile enough for me to grab him by the scruff of the neck. I managed to use a catch pole and get them all back into the cage. Must have been quite a sight for the motoring public whizzing by and watching.

There was a landowner in the Eatonville area who hated elk, hated the Game Department, hated me and the local Enforcement Agent. The elk would come into his cattle pasture and eat the grass. They also damaged his fences. I spent a lot of time at his farm herding elk and shooting M-80 cracker shells at them. All to no avail. I sprayed deer "repellant" all around his pastures. It was horrible smelling stuff but had no effect on elk. The local Fish & Wildlife Officer told me that elk fear the smell of human urine. So, for a week, every time I had to go, I would pee in a jug. Finally, I poured this into a sprayer and headed for the farm with high hopes of solving the problem. I sprayed all around a pasture thinking I was finally "gonna fix them elk" once and for all. It didn't work, not even a little bit, and the landowner called that evening and yelled about the elk in his pasture. The guy kinda reminded me of Bob and the culvert deal. Wow, what a mouth!

I had a call from a forester working for a tree farm where he had fenced in an acre of land to keep deer out and study the effects of various treatments on tree growth. He started seeing damage to some of the small trees and thought it was from mice, or something. I went out and inspected the area inside the enclosure for animal sign. There was a pile of old logs laying in the center of the enclosure and I happened to find a porcupine quill stuck in a log where something was crawling inside the pile. I told the guy he had fenced his problem in and I thought I could take care of it.

I set a #330 Conibear trap at the entrance to the hole where the quill was. The very next morning we had a large porcupine in the trap. I think that was just lucky, but I let the forester know that I was a very experienced trapper and tracker and always got my porky. He believed me.

**Raccoon Heaven**

I live-trapped a lot of skunks in the city and suburbs. I would take them out onto Fort Lewis and release them in areas where people dumped trash, hoping to deter this activity. It probably had no effect. I don't know if it was the trash or the skunks that caused the Army to fence and gate the entire area off to the public. But I'll bet they still have a healthy population of skunks out there.

Way up the North Fork of the Teanaway River there is a chunk of private land with some cabins. I've always admired one especially - a two story, very nice-looking backwoods cabin. I always had a desire to own it. On a cold February day I received a dispatch call about a problem with a bear at this cabin. Well, not at, but **in**. I called the owner and he said he would meet me with his snowmobile at the 29 Pines sno-park. The road from there up is open for snowmobile traffic only. It was a 5-mile ride to the cabin.

I had no idea what to expect until I met with the cabin owner. He said the snow was so high that a bear was able to walk up onto the roof of the cabin. Then it fell through a plastic skylight. They didn't know how long it had been there but found it there when they came up to spend the weekend. From what he could see looking in the door the place was trashed! Our bruin had made himself right at home, every inch of it.

The owner left the door open hoping the bear would just walk out. But that didn't work. Now he wanted me to figure out how to get it out. That's why I "get paid the big bucks, right?", he said, with a twisted grin on his face. So, when I stepped in the door, I startled the bear off from his nice bed on the couch. He ran into an alcove behind the wood stove to hide.

I had seen a long, three-section handled snow rake outside and asked if I could use it. I was a little nervous as this was a hungry wild bear that had been trapped in the cabin for who knows how long. Being the brave Game Warden I had to put on a good front and act like it was no big deal to go inside the cabin with this ferocious carnivore. So, in I went with my long pole for protection (yes, I did have my side arm as well).

As I got inside the living room, I could see the bear behind the stove. Leaving the door wide open I eased across the room to the sofa on the far side away from the door. From about 15 feet away I started poking the pole in behind the stove and yelling, "Ha Bear, get outta here". I could see it was a young bear, light brown colored, and he was probably scared to death. From my vantage point I could see what a mess he had made of this beautiful cabin. I didn't think I wanted to own it anymore.

I kept moving a little closer and finally got to where I could actually poke the bear in the butt. That did it! He bolted out from behind the stove, around the corner and right out the door - A blaze of brown in high speed. Good thing I had told the folks outside to stay away from the door. One of them did get a photo of him running out through the snowy woods.

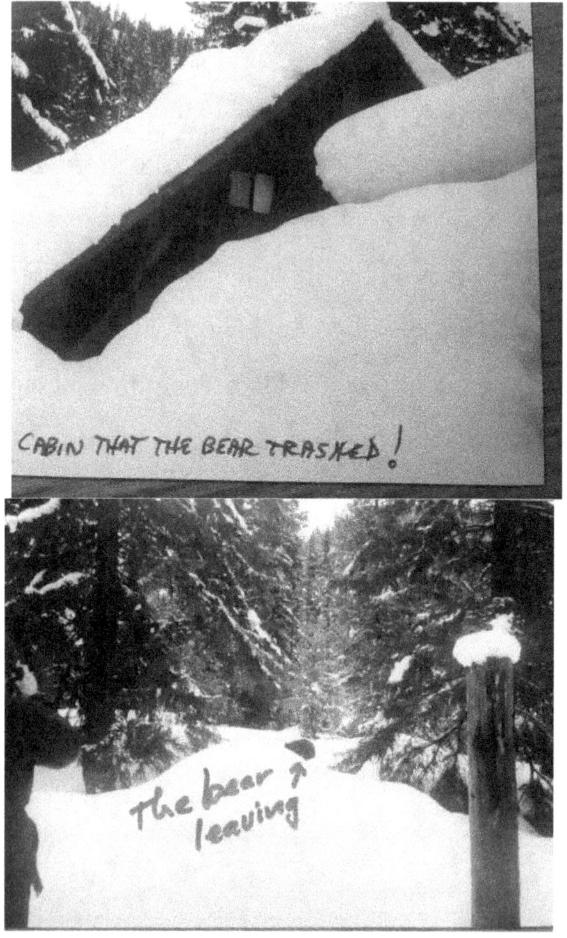



After I saved the day, we all got to take a closer look at the inside of the wonderful cabin. "Trashed" is a little understated. He had managed to use all the beds and floor space for a toilet. All the kitchen cupboards were opened and emptied. Scratches and tooth marks were on all the woodwork. The folks were pleased, thanked me profusely, and hauled me back to my vehicle. End of story? Not quite.

A few days later, and about fifteen miles away in the Middle Fork, there was a new bear complaint at another cabin. The owner lived there full time and kept a trashcan full of dog food on the front porch. Seems our light brown scoundrel had made his way here and found the dog food. I hauled the live trap up and set it with special bear bait - Twinkies. Not interested. I tried jam and honey, and other sweet, gooey stuff. The bear just kept coming back for the dog food. So, I put the whole danged can of dog food inside the trap and hooked it to the trigger.

The next morning, I had a call that we had the bear caught. Sure enough, it was the same bear from the North Fork cabin. He was skinny and in poor shape. I called the Biologist for help and he arranged for a Rehab specialist from Seattle to take him and nurse him back to health. Three months later he was released up above Yakima in a nice new home a long, long way from any cabins.

# Chapter 7 - "Dangerous Situation"

I was on patrol in the Cle Elum area one afternoon in December 1993. It had snowed and was very chilly out. I was thinking about wrapping up the day as it had been pretty slow for wildlife enforcement activity, finding only a few guys out fishing for Mountain Whitefish. I was the only Game Warden on duty in the county and there was only one Officer on duty in the town of Cle Elum. I had had coffee with him earlier and we discussed how slow things were and the impending winter storm.

At about 4 pm I heard some chatter on the radio and realized it was the Cle Elum Officer calling his dispatch about an incident in progress in town. I immediately headed his way in case he needed backup. The nearest state trooper was somewhere out on the freeway west of town near Snoqualmie Pass.

I gathered that a suspect had entered a flooring store and taken a female employee hostage at knifepoint. Two other employees had hidden in the back of the store and managed to get into the restroom and locked the door.

When I arrived at the store I started to enter, as I could see the City cop inside. He motioned for me to stop and wait. He was talking to the guy who was on the floor behind a counter with a knife to the employee's throat. He was trying to get the suspect to let her go.

What we found out later was that this same guy had been in a local motel a week before, had been sniffing glue, and was eventually put on a bus to Seattle. Now he was back and, obviously out his head again. Turns out he had family in town.

The conversation between the suspect and the officer centered on letting the hostage go and coming after the Officer. The suspect asked if the officer would shoot him if he did that. It was a "suicide by cop" kind of situation. The suspect knew he was messed up and wanted to die. The officer told him to let her go and find out if he would shoot him.

In the meantime, the county sheriff had come in the back door and managed to get the other two women outside. Also, a State Patrol Sergeant had arrived at the front door with me.

Suddenly, the city officer motioned for me to come in. Just as I entered the door I saw the suspect stand up, come around the end of the counter, and start walking straight toward us from about twenty feet. He had a large carving knife held up in his right hand. We both drew our firearms while yelling to drop the knife and stop. "Police, drop the knife!!", "get on the floor!!".

He kept coming. Training kicked in. The whole scene seemed to go into slow motion. At about ten feet the Cle Elum officer fired two shots at the guy. I fired one shot and saw him going down. We still had him covered as he lay there looking up. He asked if he was going to die? Geeez! What could I say? I didn't answer him as the EMTs rushed to his side.

The officer's shots both struck the guy in his left arm. My shot went center mass, into his chest cavity and out his back. He was shooting a .357 revolver, I had a 9mm Glock. Later on, my firearms instructor asked me why I didn't "double-tap" him like we were trained? I told him that when I fired the guy was already going down and didn't need a second shot. My hollow-point bullet didn't even mushroom till it hit the wall.

I'm glad to say the guy survived and went to prison. The city officer, the WA State Patrol sergeant, and I were hailed as heroes and given plaques, and all the ladies at the store were safe. The next week I purchased a new Glock in .45 caliber.

I was engaged to be married at the time and my future bride was at work while all this went down. She didn't know about it until I called her and gave her a quick run-down on the shooting. I had a meeting with my supervisor, then a de-briefing with a State Patrol investigator and psychologist. Finally, at about 9 pm, I stopped to see my fiancée and tell her about it. I'm sure she was wondering what the Hell she was getting into with me.  Now, after 26 years of wedded bliss, she's still wondering. Gotta keep 'em on their toes, eh? I think she was very relieved when I retired.

# Chapter 8 - "Cougar vs Goats and More"

One of our fish & wildlife Bugs, Big Game Biologist Dr. Gary Koehler, started a program with our local school system called project CAT (Cougars and Teaching). Google "project cat" to see a video. The project received huge support from the community as well as lots of funding from various sources.

The plan was for an eight-year cougar monitoring project where students would go out with Dr. Koehler and a hound hunter to tree, dart, and radio collar cougars in the upper Kittitas County area. They took tooth, blood and hair samples for aging and DNA. The collars also had GPS transmitters and over the 8 years the kids and Department computerized massive documentation on locations, travel routes, kill sites, age and health, and much more info on the cougars that were captured and studied. The kids learned a lot about wildlife management, data entry, mapping and much more.

In the beginning the Biologist did not know the area and recruited me to go along to show them how to get around and introduce them to landowners. I can say it was a great experience going out on snowshoes, travelling miles through deep snow, to find a cat up a tree. I learned a lot about the cats and their behavior and will be forever grateful for the chance. I know of at least two students who went on to become wildlife biologists.

One of the cougars we had captured was nicknamed LIMO, after two students Lisa and Monica. He was a large male and covered a huge part of the upper county. One night I was called out by Dispatch for a road-killed cougar on I-90 just west of town. It was LIMO! He was probably crossing the freeway in pursuit of a female cougar or a deer. Blinded by love or hunger, he ran right out in front of a semi-truck. Project CAT ponied up the money to have LIMO mounted and he was donated to the school where he is still on display.

One snowy, cold day the Project CAT crew decided to take some students and media to the Taneum Creek area to look for a cougar to track. I went along as a "guide". I noticed some marks in the snow along the road and we discovered a cat had cached a freshly killed deer there. The hounds were released, and they took off up the very steep hillside.

We could see tracks of an adult female and two kittens going up the hill. I think there were fifteen of us struggling up that snowy hillside, following the sounds of the hounds and following the trail. When we broke out on the top of the ridge, we found the hounds had treed two kittens. No sign of Mom.

We decided to spread out and go back down the mountain looking for the female cat. I decided to go down the same trail we went up and I just happened to look up into a large pine tree. I saw a long, tawny tail hanging down - and there was Mom. We had all walked right under her on the way up. The Biologist arrived and we determined she was too far up the tree to try darting with a tranquilizer as she might fall too far to the ground. It was an exciting chase, and the media folks got a great story and photos.

A couple years after the project ended, I received a call about a cougar killing goats near town. I called and then met with the landowners to see what had happened. They had three pet goats in a small, enclosed area with a 4-foot-high fence. It worked great for keeping the goats in but not so well for keeping things like cougars out.

Two of the goats had been killed and one taken out of the enclosure. In searching the brushy area nearby, I finally found the missing goat covered up in thick brush. Luckily no sign of the cat.

I called one of the project CAT biologists to see if I could borrow their cougar live trap. He was willing to bring it up from the Ellensburg office for me and helped set it up just outside the goat pen. I dragged the dead goat from the brush, leaving a good scent trail, and into the back of the live trap.

Then I had a long chat with the goat owners. I explained that the area has more cougars than most people know, explaining the results of the Project CAT. When you place a "food source" like goats out where a cat can get to them, they certainly will get to them. I recommended they build a much higher fence and consider putting the goats inside a shed at night. Also, I said I didn't know if we could catch the offending cougar but would give it a try.

The very next morning I had a call from the landowner saying we caught a cougar in the trap. I was elated and drove straight to their place. Sure enough, there was a young Tom inside the trap. He was a two-year-old male. Unfortunately, the Department's policy on livestock killing predators is that they must be euthanized. I called the biologist, and he came to help me. We put the cat down and took tooth and blood samples. This information would be entered into the project CAT data base.

The sad thing is that many "city" people move to this area for the rural living experience. They don't realize there are predatory animals nearby (cougars, bobcats, bears, coyotes, and now wolves). They want to have a small ranch with some animals, like pet cats and dogs running loose, goats, sheep, llamas, and such. Often times these pets come up missing and the people call the Fish & Wildlife Department for help. And often times all we can do is give them advice on protecting their animals better.

I knew a little old lady outside of town in a very rural area. She and her family had been there several generations and knew all about living in the wilds. She was a real sweetheart and often gave me jars of handpicked and preserved wild strawberry jam. She was a widow, lived alone and managed quite well with chores and keeping her firewood stacked in a small shed out back behind her house.

One morning, to her great surprise, she came around the corner of the shed to get some wood and was face-to-face with a cougar. It was sitting on top of the wood pile and snarled at her. She ran for the house and called me directly. She said, "Goodness gracious, I didn't know what to do. Should I shoot it?"

I told her to stay in the house and I would be right out. When I got there, she was waiting at the front door. I grabbed a shotgun, loaded up some OO buckshot, and carefully walked around the side of the house to the woodshed. I made a quick peek inside and saw the cat. It looked very skinny and small - I figured it was just a yearling and, without an adult to care for it, it was not eating well. When I turned around, I almost bumped into the homeowner - she was standing right behind me! Kinda spooked me and made me jump. Not nervous or anything!

I told her that the cat was very sick and skinny, and I would probably need to put it down. She said that was fine with her, "just do it". I told her to go back in the house. I shot the cat and, after checking the body, I could tell it would not have lasted much longer this winter. I dragged it around to the front door and took a picture of her looking out at it. This could have had a tragic outcome had she gone closer into the woodshed.

# Chapter 9 - "Hunting Accidents"

Under the old Game Department, we used the term "Hunting Accident" when someone was hurt, as in being shot, during the hunting seasons. Since then that term has been changed to "hunting incident", since shooting someone by "accident" should never happen. Firearms are only dangerous in the hands of people who do not follow good safety procedures and, in the case of hunting, knowing your target and what lies beyond it.

My very first deer hunting season in the Cle Elum area was an eye opener. It seemed like everyone, and I mean everyone, from the Westside of the state came to Cle Elum to hunt deer. It was opening day in the Teanaway River Valley and I was awestruck at the numbers of hunters and the locations and size of camps - they were everywhere! There was one camp up the North Fork with eight RVs and a couple wall tents. There was a huge campfire ring and I think these guys were mainly there for a gathering rather than deer hunting. There were always a dozen or so of them standing around the fire.

About halfway through the day I had a radio call of a hunting accident in the area of Johnson Creek, up the North Fork of the Teanaway River. A hunter was standing by at the trailhead waiting for someone to help. I wasn't too far away and met with the person within about 15 minutes.

The weather was cold and wet with more rain threatening. The person told me a guy had been shot in the legs and was about a mile and half up the trail. I had never been up Johnson Creek Trail and did not know the lay of the land. I called for assistance from the County Sheriff's Office and for medical aid. I also requested some Search and Rescue people to respond to help transport the injured victim out.

I told the guy at the trailhead to remain there and direct the other responding folks to the area. He told me he was glad to do that and said there were some people at the scene that knew first aid. Also, he told me that the guy that did the shooting was waiting there.

I grabbed a pack with first aid gear, water and food, and headed up the trail. My head was spinning in high-speed wondering how this could have happened and how I was going to handle it. My priority would be helping the victim. Secondly, I would need to interview the shooter and get the full story for the investigation.

It was a grueling hike up this trail with slippery rocks and tree roots. Upon arriving at the scene, I found a group of people helping calm the victim, as he was in a great deal of pain and very unhappy with his situation. As he was being well attended, I turned my attention to the shooter. He was a nice young man and was very remorseful about what had happened. I told him I had a Sheriff's Deputy coming up but would like to have a quick idea of what happened.

The poor guy was almost in tears as he tried to relate his side of it. He said it was his first-time hunting deer and his friend and hunting partner had gone up a different hillside. As he was walking up the trail, he said he saw legs in the brush. Although the legs were covered in blue denim, he was sure it was a deer. He apparently didn't realize the season was open for buck deer only. He said he thought he could "shoot it in the legs and it would jump out in the open so he could get a better shot" (his words). As soon as the shot went off, he heard some loud screaming and realized what had happened.

I collected the guy's hunting license and ID and told him to stand by. As I was checking on the victim, I saw Deputy Swanson arriving with some EMT's and other people coming to help. I gave the shooter's ID to Swanson and had him continue the investigation while I organized the group to help carry out the victim. Fish & Wildlife Officer Jeff Sweezy arrived, and we helped get the victim on a gurney and started packing him out. It was a long and arduous trip down the steep trail and the poor guy on the gurney did a lot of screaming. One of the EMT's from the ambulance was Donna Willette, my future Mother-in-Law.  Go figure. I met her under these circumstances and way before I met her daughter.

It turned out the victim was shot through both legs just above the knees. He survived and healed with no lasting problems. Although, I felt he probably would have problems with pain and arthritis in his older years.

As in most hunting accidents involving someone being shot, the shooter lost his hunting privilege in Washington for life, as well in other States involved in the Interstate Wildlife Violator Compact. After 10 years he could appeal to get his hunting privilege back.

Several years later I had to investigate a man who was shot in the right rear cheek by his son with a .50 caliber muzzleloader. The son thought he saw a cow elk moving through the nearby brush. It turned out to be his father sneaking up on an elk. He was wearing brown canvass pants.

All 50 States have a Hunter Education Program, partly funded by Federal money under the Pittman-Robertson Act. These programs have become required for all hunters born after Jan. 1st, 1972. They follow a standard program nationwide and I have taught the Enforcement portion of the classes for over 35 years. With my years of experience, I can relate many examples of people doing "stupid things" out in the woods with firearms. It is very rewarding to be able to help young people, new hunters, learn about firearm safety, ethics, wildlife management, wildlife identification, seasons, bag limits, etc. This program is generally run by volunteers who want to help educate our youth. This is also where I met my future Father-in-Law, Jim Willette, who had helped teach Hunter Education classes, through the Cascade Field & Stream Club, for over 20 years with his Brother Tom and former Cle Elum Mayor Mike Rosetti. Also, way before I met my future Bride.

# Chapter 10 - "Game Warden's wife's side of it"

## The Best Game Warden Wife

As I was retiring in July 2011 my wife, Cindy, was busy planning a gathering and festivities. She sat down and wrote the following essay with the intention of reading it at the retirement party. Many of us know how fond Cindy is about getting up in front of a crowd and reading anything - NOT! So, she just gave it to me to read and I thought it should be included here, especially because she said nice things about me:

## The Game Warden's Wife by Cindy Rogers

My life with my game warden husband, Steve, has been a wonderful learning, creative experience. Thank goodness we both share such a love of the great outdoors. Hunting, fishing, boating, hiking, camping anywhere and everywhere, has made it one huge adventure. In other words, if you know Steve, he is a colorful character that makes life a whole lotta fun!! And although an overused statement, "Never a dull moment". It is all about us.

My Dad, who was a little soft-spoken, met Steve (besides everywhere in a small town) in the Hunter Education classes. Dad taught them for 20 plus years here in Cle Elum. After Steve and I were engaged Dad said, "He is a good man". That packed a wallop of a compliment and said all there was to say.

And my husband is a good man. I have watched him during his career, and he has handled himself with honesty and fairness. In our Upper County area many people in wildlife predicaments demanded "Call Steve". "We want Steve". And Steve would go and unravel whatever he could. Same with the many knocks on our door and "I need help" or "I have a question". No one was ever turned away.

Through some long worrisome nights and of course long hunting seasons I said some "keep him safe" prayers. And said a few "thank yous" when he did arrive home safe. But Steve loved his job and always came home with good stories and a smile. And lots of "I got 'ems".

Each year I would give the hunting season a nickname. Like the year of the bear. Each year had its groupings of things that happened. One year, the "year of the bear", Steve set the live trap 5 times, trapping a total of 5 orphaned bear cubs. Steve used Twinkies in the big green bear trap on wheels. Each time a little bear, a different size and color. I made a mental note to not take Twinkies with us camping, hiking, or hunting.

**Unhappy cub in the live trap**

Then there was the year of the elk, a pickup bed full of elk antlers and carcasses. There was herding elk with snowmobiles through the one-way "return gates" on the elk fence around the valley. And elk stuck in everything, their antlers tangled in cables, fences, tow ropes, waiting for Steve to cut them loose. That tow rope elk kicked his (rhymes with grass). And that's all I'm going to say about that.

Steve came home with a variety of animals. Some live, some not. That was the time to call the family and down they would come with their cameras. I hope the nieces and nephews will remember. People would call him and report their finds - illegal kills, bull elk, bears, cougars, hawks, eagles, deer and beaver. He didn't bring them all home, thank goodness, but only what he needed to use for educational purposes or evidence. Another extension of the love he has for the wildlife and the outdoors.

Our families, his and mine, are all proud of Steve. His years of dependable service, sharing his stories with us (and his jokes), his "talking" version of the rules and "regs". We could ask all the questions we wanted, and argue all we wanted with our own "Gamey". We are very proud of you, honey! I'm sure my Dad enjoyed pulling your chain about the stupid "catch and release" rules on the river, too.

Being the wife of a wildlife officer is an incredible experience. I was the only wife where I worked that got all-weather hunting camo clothing for the holiday season and rifle scopes for my birthday. I loved it.

So, congratulations Steve, Wildlife 125, from 125.5 (your better half). Happy retirement and thank you for the memories.

Love, Cindy

**Cindy on Ol' No Name with faithful friends, Shep and Babe**

# Chapter 11 - "Elk do the darndest things"

I've seen a whole lifetime of bad things that happen to wild animals. For example, I worked at the Whidbey Island Game Farm when I was first hired. We raised pheasants, starting from picking up eggs in the nests in fields, to incubating the eggs, and then raising the chicks in sheds with heated hoods. It was terrible to find the many ways these poor little chicks could kill themselves, from getting stuck in the chicken wire over the windows, to hanging up under the hoods in the electrical wires, to drowning in their water dishes. Then we put them out in the fields with wing bands and the owls and eagles would have a heyday.

We've all seen road kills where deer and elk, raccoons, bears and even beaver try to cross busy roads and get schwacked.

I had a call from my Park Ranger buddy from Lake Easton State Park. He was manager of the former Iron Horse Trail, now Pouluse to Mountains Trail, on the old Milwaukie Railroad right-of-way that goes through Kittitas County. His calls were always interesting and sometimes just crazy. Seems he had a crew of helpers taking down old power lines along the trail and, while unattended, some of the wires were hanging near the ground.

This happened to be in September and the bull elk were rutting - it was breeding season. Apparently, a large bull elk had decided to fight with some old power lines and got himself a little wrapped up in his business.

The trail is a non-motorized system but the Ranger gave me permission to drive to the location of the distressed elk. By the time I got there we had quite a large group of hikers who had found the elk and hoped to see how it was resolved. The bull, a large 7x7, was so tightly wrapped up in the wires that he could not move. He had managed to wind around some small trees and had his head snubbed up tight against one of them. He looked exhausted but had fire in his eyes as I approached to assess the situation - definitely not a happy camper, mad with lust and downright hatred for me.

It appeared I had two options for a solution here. One was to shoot the derned thing. Or, two, cut him loose. I didn't like either option but headed for my toolbox and my trusty fencing pliers. I thought, if this brute got loose, he could run right over that little tree and me with no effort. But I had an audience and felt I should look brave and do something for this magnificent, albeit stupid, elk. Some may have called me stupid as well, but I was *The Game Warden*.

So, I eased up on him, facing him straight on. His eyes got redder, if that was possible. I reached out and started snipping the wires that I could get ahold of. Here a careful snip, there another. The minutes dragged on. I was sweating profusely. All of a sudden, I got the right wire, and the elk went flying backward, away from me. He just stood there, about ten feet away. I'm sure he was totally exhausted and couldn't move. There was still a little nest of wire in his antlers but at least he was free.

The audience started clapping and yelling. I slowly backed away from the elk and asked the people to please be quiet and let him get his bearings. I was still a little shaky and sweating. I had everyone leave and I drove down the trail a few yards and parked to make sure the elk left. It took about 20 minutes, but he finally started off toward the forest. I called my park ranger buddy and told him to handle this sort of thing himself next time and to buy himself a good pair of fencing pliers. Again, I could write another book just on my escapades with this Ranger, including turkey and duck hunting, death marches and many other tall tales.

I had a similar call on a private ranch near Cle Elum where a large bull elk had become entwined in some old fencing. Again, he had cleared a swath about ten feet around himself and was snubbed up to a fir tree. I knew the landowner, Harvey, well, and having lots of experience with this sort of thing, I told him no problem, I'd just go in there and cut him loose. Harvey stayed up in his Gator on the road and told me to be careful. No sweat, right?

The smooth wire fencing was thicker than the old power line I had cut easily before. This time I had to use both hands on the pliers and each snip made a loud noise that, in turn, made the bull very nervous. He jumped and I jumped! My face was inches from those long, sharp antler tines and I was sweating in spite of the 15-degree temperature and snow on the ground.

I made some progress, and the elk was able to move a little bit. That made me even more nervous, and I actually wondered if I would survive this one. Finally, I cut through a piece of wire and the bull stood straight up and looked at me. I took off running up the hill to the road and safety. The bull turned around and ran off into the woods. Harvey was taking pictures of the whole thing and laughing his head off (he's an old cowboy with a great sense of humor). That bull ended up shedding his antlers the next spring, across the valley on another ranch, and they were still wrapped in barbed wire.

I was summoned to Snoqualmie Pass and a ski resort area on yet another elk caper. This time a bull had become entangled with the tow rope on one of the ski runs. Great, I thought, just what I need. It was cold and windy, some snow on the ground, and a whole lot of mud. His antlers were entwined in a small rope attached to the larger tow rope. The manager pleaded with me to please do not cut the big rope. I thought, "yeah, whatever - you go cut him loose".

As I worked my way down the rope to the elk he started pulling backward. He was as far back as he could get, and that rope was taut! I pulled out my trusty Kershaw knife and started to work on the small rope. I could see it was wrapped many times around all of his tines. When I cut the critical piece holding him everything seemed to go into slow motion. And then, I went flying. The main rope caught me and flung me 15 feet back into a big mud hole and the elk ran off the other direction. My only thought was, "what the Hell am I doing here? Stupid elk!" I was soaked to the skin and covered in mud. When I got home, I had to undress in the garage before the wife would let me in the house.

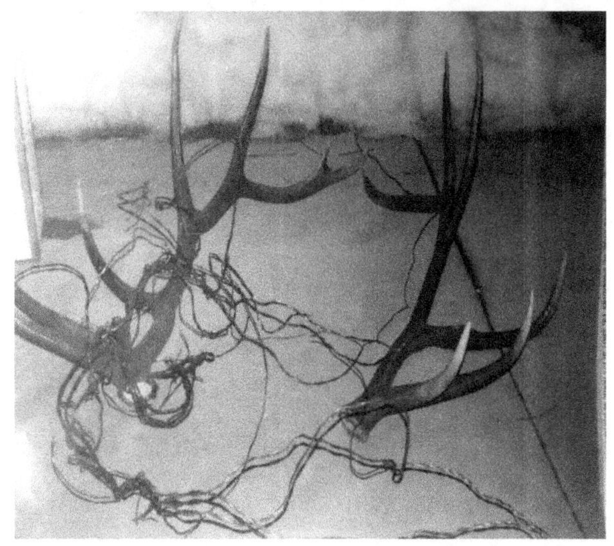

**Shed elk antlers with wire still wrapped on**

I found a calf elk caught in a fence once and had to figure out how to release him. When I managed to cut him loose, he stepped back and gave me this crazy look, as if to say, "what? You never seen a calf elk before?" "Now leave me alone!"

# Chapter 12 - "Elk Season"

Back around 1999, give or take, I wrote up a story for the Washington Game Warden Association Newsletter, *The Informant.* I think Todd Vandivert was the editor back then. An accomplished author, Todd actually printed my story instead of sending it back with a rejection letter. I'll reproduce it here for your reading pleasure:

Opening day of elk season - where to go first? When you have a huge area to patrol combined with a large elk population and about half of Western Washington is over here looking for them, do you suppose there is a potential for fateful mishaps? So, everyone knows that the Game Warden is on top of things and knows the right place and time to be in the action. Well, this year I had lots of potential problem areas to work on opening day and I picked Cooper Lake/Cooper Pass.

Cooper Lake is a beautiful high lake at the edge of the Alpine Lake Wilderness. You can drive along the East side of the lake, past Owhi Campground and end up at the Trailhead to the wilderness area or drive up the West side to Cooper Pass and over into Honolulu Basin above Lake Kachess. Right at the upper end of Cooper Lake is a large meadow along the Cooper River where elk use a small pond and wet area for wallows. There is also a clearcut next to the meadow. This area is heavily used by elk and is visible from the Cooper Pass Road. The clearcut is accessible from a small logging spur which winds down the hill to a landing in the middle of the clearcut.

So, opening morning, like the dedicated Game Warden that I am, I'm sitting on Cooper Pass an hour before legal shooting time waiting to hear shots before legal time. By ten minutes before shooting time I had yet to even see a vehicle or any sign of human activity. Self-doubt began to creep into my psyche. I'm thinking I could have headed down to the Colockum Wildlife Area, or over to Elk Heights. But, no, here I am with no activity.

But I could see a group of elk down in the clearcut. With my spotting scope I could see a large 6x6 bull, 2 legal spikes, and a dozen or so cows and calves, all feeding about 50 yards from the landing. The season was open for spikes only. A spike bull has at least one antler that does not branch or fork.

Finally, at about 15 minutes after shooting time, a jeep came up the road with two guys dressed head-to-toe in orange. I'm sitting on the edge of the logging road with a spotting scope on my window pointed down at the clearcut. They waved and went on by! What? They weren't curious as to what I was looking at. After another ten minutes I decided I had picked the wrong spot, cussed myself a little, and headed down the road.

Just around the next corner there is another hunter, solid orange, standing in the road with a video camera. When I contacted him, he asked if I had seen that large bull down there. I politely told him I had, that it was a 6x6 bull. He must have had a Helluva zoom on that camera because we were a good half mile away from the elk. I asked him if he had seen the two spikes that were standing about 20 yards from the bull. Needless to say, he had not. He went crazy, like many elk hunters do when they see elk, and started grabbing his gear. I told him where the spur road was and that, if he went part way down it and walked the rest of the way down, he would come out right where those elk were feeding. This guy took off driving down the spur road about 90mph, skidded to a stop and slammed his door when he got out. The elk moved a little farther back in the brush.

Just then the two fellers in the jeep came back down the main road. I stepped out and got them to stop. I asked if they were hunting elk, they said they were, and they asked the question, "where ya got 'em tied up?" I said I wasn't exactly hiding them and that, if they would look around some they just might see elk, including those two spikes down there in the clearcut.

Whoa! Elk!! They jumped out with their rifles and started "scoping" down at the elk. I asked them, politely, to stop doing that because there was another hunter down there and I didn't want to have to investigate a hunting incident. The one guy thought he could hit one of those elk from there. I suggested he not do that or I would write him up for shooting off a public road and possibly reckless endangerment.

Just then we could see the other hunter walking down through the trees on the spur road and out to the landing, rifle slung over his shoulder. The elk moved a little farther into the brush.

After two or three minutes he turned around and walked back to the road, having seen no elk. That was too much for these other two hunters. I told them how to get down the spur road and the same strategy I had given the first guy. I really wanted to check some elk today and not have the whole day wasted.

Did I mention they had lost their muffler earlier that morning? They took off down the road sounding like a freight train while the elk continued feeding and looking up to watch. Instead of stopping at the other hunter's rig these guys figured they would just barrel their way down and jump the elk. They roared all the way down to the landing, jumped out slamming both doors, and split up, running into the clearcut. The elk stepped a little farther into the brush and stood there watching while these two yahoos combed their way into the brush. The hunters came together at a large stump and both climbed up on it for a better look. I watched all of the elk turn and cross the river into the jungle and away from these crazy people. The two hunters never saw them.

I shook my head and got back into my patrol truck. I headed back down the road thinking I had seen enough and there weren't going to be any dead elk to check here today. Another rig came up the road with four orange-clad hunters in it. They flagged me over and said they hadn't seen any elk all morning (ALL morning? - it is now about 45 minutes after legal shooting time) and wondered if I had an idea where any elk might be? I just smiled and said, "I haven't seen a thing either, good luck".

**By Bruce Richards, Retired Gamie and fantastic photographer**

# Chapter 13 - "The Great Teanaway Elk Caper" "Or Sometimes They Get Away"

Anyone who has read through the Washington Fish and Wildlife Hunting regulations pamphlet over the last ten years or so has probably seen this photo of yours truly investigating a poached bull elk. I never got any royalties from their use of my picture, but I want to give credit where it is due - Cle Elum local sportsman and Cascade Field & Stream member, Bob Bailey, took the "money shot" that should have made both of us wealthy. Oh, well, I digress.

During the 2005 early archery elk season a herd of elk had been chased down into the Teanaway River farmlands and on to a property where hunting was not allowed. Lots of people were driving by taking pictures and admiring the several large bulls in the group. Eventually they left this field and went over to a different hay field nearby. All but one. There was one nice 6-point bull laying in the field and he did not get up and run with the others. That was when the landowner called me because the elk was obviously hurt.

When I arrived a half hour later the bull had died. It had a wound on its left side, but I could not tell what kind of wound until I cut the hide back. When I did this, I found what looked like a broadhead arrow tip wound. It appeared the arrow had gone all the way through and out the other side, slicing through vital organs and causing death. It was actually a well-placed shot. The problem was that the elk ran onto private property before dying. My thought was that the hunter was scared to follow the elk onto this private property for fear of getting caught trespassing. My other thought was that he could have located the landowner and asked for permission to pursue his wounded elk. But then, maybe he did not have a license or elk tag. Who knows?

So, there I was with a large dead elk in the middle of a hay field visible on three sides from public roads with lots of people gawking. And an upset landowner asking what I'm going to do about it.

The fourth side of the field was river bottom along the Teanaway River. It was brushy and thick with Cottonwood trees. I was told that was the direction the herd came from. I thought the suspect's arrow may be somewhere in that brush.

A neighbor, whom I have known for years, came out to the field with his tractor, along with several other locals. We managed to hoist the elk up, get him field dressed, and loaded into my truck. Hence the photo of me calling it in and asking if the Union Gospel Mission was available to come get it.

I asked the group if I could get any volunteers to sort through the brush to look for the arrow. After about an hour we gave up, having found nothing of use.

The story basically ends here. I had no evidence and no suspect. I was very frustrated, and all the locals were furious. Sometimes we just can't make a case and it drives me crazy thinking about it. It's one thing to make a case and lose it in court. But, to have nothing to go on and no witnesses, there just isn't much more to do.

A couple of years later I heard of another large bull shot and left up near the town of Ronald. The bull in question was one of three that hung around a housing area just north of town and all the neighbors loved seeing them. They were kind of like pets.

One early morning one of these bulls was found lying in a clearing near the highway. When I arrived, it was already starting to bloat. It must have been killed at very first light that morning. My sergeant arrived to help, and we looked over the bull. When we rolled it over, we found an arrow hanging out of the offside.

By the time we did our investigation and took DNA samples and photos it was too late to salvage the meat. The elk was loaded and taken to a pit at the Department of Transportation where they dump road kills. What a shame to see this magnificent animal just dumped into a hole. We did save the antlers for evidence and eventually displayed them at our Detachment office.

We had no suspects and no witnesses. I wrote an article in the local newspaper asking for any help or information on this poaching case. I did receive several calls on possible suspects, but nothing panned out. I think some of the locals would have turned in their own mother if they thought she had done this horrible thing.

I did some checking on the arrow trying to find where it had been sold. It had the manufacturer's name and a lot number. But the company was unable to tell where it had been sold, much less who bought it.

The long and short of it is that we never made a case. It was probably an opportunist who saw the bull from the road and took a potshot at it with a bow. Or, it may have been shot somewhere else and wandered out to where it died. This sort of stuff is what keeps game wardens awake at night, wondering what if I had just………

# Chapter 14 - "Taxidermists"

This photo is still being used in the Washington Fish and Wildlife Hunting Regulations pamphlet and I still don't get any royalties! But it shows a sad picture of what happens when a taxidermist doesn't follow the rules. All items in the truck were seized for forfeiture and later destroyed or used for educational purposes. There are many great Taxidermists who are professional and do fabulous work to display wildlife specimens. We usually do annual inspections of their ledgers and sometimes they would call us with possible violation information.

I received a call from a friend in Roslyn telling me that he had sent his trophy bull elk head to a Taxidermist and had never gotten it back or had a call that it was ready to pick up. He had called the business several times and got no answer or return call. I remembered when he had been drawn for the special permit and had actually checked his bull after he brought it home. He was understandably upset.

I had had some other reports of this Taxidermist doing suspicious activity but nothing much I could follow up on. This missing elk head was something I would definitely check on.

I called the business number for this Taxidermist and had no answer and no recording to leave a message. I went to the address twice hoping to catch someone there. He had a sign on his gate with his business name and phone number. The gate was closed and locked. I checked with Olympia headquarters and learned his Taxidermy License had not been renewed that year. The third time I went to the address I took my Sergeant along. The gate to his place was closed and we hopped over it to go knock on the door. Still no response. We did see several deer heads with antlers attached on top of a shed. We could see no tags attached to them. I left my business card on his workshop door with a note for him to call me.

In the meantime, we discussed what to do next. I decided we had enough information to request a search warrant. Due to the fact that we saw sets of deer antlers that appeared to be fresh (from the past hunting season) and that he had not renewed his license, we went to the Prosecuting Attorney's Office and discussed it with him. He agreed that a Judge would probably authorize a search warrant and we got to work on it.

I had to fill out an affidavit showing probable cause that a crime had been committed, ie. Possessing multiple sets of antlers from other people without a valid Taxidermy license. (He obviously could not have taken several deer himself). Also, that he had a set of elk antlers from the guy in Roslyn. The actual search warrant form would authorize us to search the shop and house, freezers, other outbuildings and vehicles for evidence of conducting taxidermy, including all required ledgers/logbooks.

I finally got a phone call from the Taxidermist who said he had been gone fishing and would be home for a few days. I made an appointment to meet with him, got the warrant signed by a judge, and I organized a group of Officers to execute the warrant. Long story short, almost everything in his shop was undocumented in his ledger, including the set of elk antlers we were looking for. Many items he claimed were his own personal property but there were no tags or other documentation to prove it. And anything in his taxidermy business must be documented in the ledger. I'll give him one thing - he was cooperative and polite. In spite of the fact, we were taking everything in his shop as evidence he kept apologizing and claiming ignorance of the rules. As we were leaving with a whole pickup full of his antlers, hides, heads, etc. he said he would probably get out of this business and stick to fishing. I told him to be sure to get his fishing license and have it with him in case we checked him out on the water. He laughed - he *did* have a sense of humor.

# Chapter 15 - "Habitual Offender"

I'm sure every Game Warden has at least one habitual offender, or as some of us say, "a frequent flyer", in his/her patrol district. This is someone who just can't keep from violating hunting and fishing regulations and can't seem to keep from getting caught.

One guy in particular was a young man who loved to be outdoors and really enjoyed fishing and hunting. He had been in some trouble and was now a convicted felon, which prohibited him from owning or possessing a firearm. Therefore, he claimed to be an archery hunter.

My first contact with him was on the local river where we had a catch and release rule for trout. The rule also required fishers to use a single, barbless hook, and bait was prohibited. So, basically it was a fly-fishing river.

I was out checking for fishing activity one day and saw a guy standing on the riverbank holding a spinning rod. From a distance with binoculars, I watched him for a while. Eventually, he reeled his line in, grabbed a jar of salmon eggs, and rebaited his hook. As he cast the line into the river I drove up and walked out to him.

I asked to see his fishing license, which he proudly produced. Then I asked if he had any idea what river he was fishing in. He said he wasn't sure, and he was pretty new to the area. So, I explained the rules, had him reel in, and cited him for the barbed hook and bait. He said he was sorry, that he didn't know the rules, and that it wouldn't happen again.

Just about a year later, and very near the same location, I found him fishing with bait again. This time he said he had forgotten the bait rule and was sorry. The problem was that I had been watching him and had seen him catch and keep two trout and put them on a stringer about 20 yards upstream amongst some brush. He denied they were his. The third time I caught him on the river he said, "Man, you're probably really mad at me". I just said, "Not at all, you're really good for business".

I had received some complaints that this guy had been hunting archery season with a rifle. Over a period of nearly 10 years, I was never able to catch him red-handed doing this, a very frustrating fact of life. I did find him driving on a closed road system once, and another time driving up through a locked gate from a closed road system (this time he had a key, a duplicate DNR fire key - He refused to say where he got it). I cited him the second time for Trespassing.

After I retired, I told my replacement officer about this guy and said he should put some effort into catching him. I told him how I had been close, but not close enough, to getting him in a big game violation. One day he received a report of possible illegal bear baiting on some private property near town. Hunting bear with bait has been outlawed in our state for many years.

The new kid, as I called him, was able to sneak into the reported location and found the ground covered with Froot Loops cereal. He saw a trail camera on a nearby tree. He began surveilling the area watching for the suspect's vehicle.

Sure enough, one morning, he saw the vehicle parked just down the road. He snuck into the bait area and caught the guy red-handed with a rifle. He ended up citing him for hunting bear over bait and for being a felon in possession of a firearm.  He called to tell me what happened, and I offered to buy him a case of beer.

When I first came to the Cle Elum area, I was told by some locals that one guy in the area liked to hunt grouse all year and didn't believe in the bag limits. I was told he had a whole freezer full of grouse. I never could catch the sneaky bugger and he eventually passed away. His freezer was probably still full of grouse.

Some well-meaning citizens would tell me things they suspected about a person but never had any information I could use to get a case going. Sometimes they would even tell me that they would report a poacher unless they thought he needed the meat to feed his family. My pat answer to that was that it may have been different back 40 years ago, but with public assistance and food banks, it is a whole new ball game today. Anyone poaching today is just that, a poacher, who steals from the rest of the honest, license buying sportspeople. Thieves are just thieves, whether they are stealing money, cars, or our precious wildlife resources.

# Chapter 16 - "Dangerous Wildlife Response Team"

In late summer of 2004, a large range fire erupted in Chelan County. It was dubbed the "Fischer Fire" and the County was asking for assistance from outside agencies like Fish & Wildlife to help with roadblocks and other public safety related activities.

I was sent up from Cle Elum to help coordinate some of the other wildlife officers with the promise of overtime pay. Several of us were registered to stay in a nice hotel in Leavenworth with per diem for meals.

The first couple of days I was assigned to be in uniform, in my marked patrol truck, and helping to block people from entering the fire zone. We worked several long days but had not received enough hours to qualify for overtime. By the fourth day the people in charge advised they did not need us anymore and we were to head home.

That was when one of our Sergeants received a call from the fire bosses that a small black bear had been seen running through an area where the fire was still raging. The report said the bear appeared to be hurt. The area was still actively burning and there were long lines of firefighters in the area. The quick-thinking

Sergeant decided this was a dangerous situation where firefighters on the line could be attacked by the bear.

The Sergeant called me on the radio and asked if I was "available" to help. I told him I was and that two other guys were also available. He told us to meet him at the fire headquarters for a briefing.

We met inside the headquarters command post, looked over maps, and developed a plan. The Sarge requested we be issued Nomex fire retardant clothing, and we were directed to the quartermaster to be outfitted. We discussed the dire situation and decided it needed a name. It was agreed we would become the "Fischer Fire Dangerous Wildlife Response Team". We donned our new uniforms, put our badges and duty belts on, and grabbed our shotguns with slugs. Truth be told, we would probably have been fired, or at least reprimanded, for being "out of uniform". But, since the Sarge was in charge.........

We headed to the commissary and got free sack lunches. We were now ready to go into the fire line and save everyone from this dangerous, and injured, bear. Never mind that no other reports had been called in and nobody had seen the bear since the first sighting. We felt this was necessary for everyone's safety.

We teamed up and drove two vehicles into the active fire area.
We decided to go to the original sighting location and take it from
there. We got out and walked in formation across a burned over
area, still smoking, looking for "sign". We could see some of the
firefighters watching us and shaking their heads. Well, we found
no "sign" and decided to split up and drive around the area looking
for the bear. Every fire vehicle we came to we asked if they had
seen anything of the bear. No luck there and we kept looking. After
milking this overtime gig for five hours the Sergeant started getting
nervous and called off the search. We had all managed to polish
off our lunches and had nothing else to do. We thanked the fire
bosses for their assistance and headed for the barn. We never heard
one word from Olympia HQ or anywhere else about this extra
detail and it went down my history book as a good, well planned
and executed operation with no injuries and no complaints. Also,
the Statute of Limitations is well past by now. I kept the uniform
for future use in bear/fire situations.

Rogers - Loaded
For Bear!!

# Chapter 17 - "Beaver Damage Control"

I started trapping beaver over in Tacoma/Pierce County area back in the early '80s. I cut my way through miles of thick brush, waded in lots of swamps, pulled/dug/blasted lots of beaver dams in creeks, including the inlet creek to the South Tacoma Trout Hatchery. Beaver are very enterprising critters and have the ability to rebuild a dam, or at least plug a hole, overnight. I have cussed them and admired them and realized there was no shortage of them.

Year after year I would have complaints of beaver damming and flooding waterways in the same places and a few new ones.

They can, at times, be very difficult to catch and it can take a great deal of time and energy to wage war against them. There is a sportsmen's club with a shooting range just south of Thunn Airfield near Puyallup, Washington. The trap range has a small spring-fed creek running just beyond the trap houses and the beaver had decided it looked like a good place to call home. They had built a dam along the creek and the resultant lake was flooding the trap houses.

The trouble with this spot was the thick cattails, wild rose and willow that bordered the creek. I could hear water rushing over a beaver dam somewhere in that thicket, but it was difficult to locate. It was a hot summer with loads of mosquitos. After fighting my way in with a machete and wading in thigh-high water, I found the dam and tore a hole in it to drain the flooded area. On returning the next morning I found the hole repaired and even improved. The club manager said he thought there was another dam downstream in the thicker part of the creek bed.

I worked on tearing holes in the two dams for a week and realized it was a waste of time. I set some traps but had no luck over the next several days. In the meantime, the club President wrote a mean letter to the Department Director complaining about what a poor job I was doing and demanding better help. I wanted to take him into that swamp and leave him with the beaver! After receiving a call from my supervisor, I decided it was time to recruit a professional beaver trapper. George Sovie, President of the State Trappers Assn., agreed to come out and help. We set three Conibear traps and, within two days we had removed four beaver. Sovie thought that would do it so I tore out the dams again.

I explained to the club folks that, since this creek spills into the Puyallup River, there will always be a beaver problem here. Working with them and our Habitat Biologist, a dredging and cleanout project was planned, and a rotating screen system was installed near the culvert to the river. This combination seemed to take care of the problem for good and I never had to go back into that mess of a "wetland".

I have lost my balance on a beaver dam and fallen into the pond, been mostly lost in a willow swamp trying to find a dam, and got my wrist caught in a #330 Conibear trap.

That trap was almost the worst thing that ever happened in my career, but it did not break my wrist. I was about 100 yards from my truck, up to my hips in water, and my feet were mired down in mud. I set the trap in a side channel. As I reached down to remove just one more twig away from the trap, I lost my balance and my hand went straight into the trigger! The trap closed on my wrist. My first thought was, "OH, man, this is gonna start to hurt". I had to get the pliers out of my pocket to cut the wire holding the trap to the stakes. Then, with a length of rope I managed to pull the springs enough to get the safety hooks on and release my hand. Then I drove about 45 minutes to the nearest clinic for x-rays. After being treated I decided it was time for a cold beer and headed home.

My Ranger Buddy from Lake Easton State Park called to tell me he had a beaver dam under a foot bridge on the hiking trail. He said the water was high, almost flooding the bridge, and wondered if I would take a look.

Unbeknownst to him I had been dealing with this particular dam spot for years because the flooding affected a small hay field just upstream. It was difficult to trap beaver there due to the volume of people using the trail. One year I had brought a canoe in to get me farther back from the trail so I could set traps more easily and safely.

The ranger asked if I could use a live trap closer to the trail and he would help me monitor it to save me going out every morning. Together, we found a suitable spot for the live trap, a large basket-type setup that would scoop a beaver up when it swims into the bait. We disguised the trap, so it wasn't very visible. I showed the Ranger how I mix up my special "stink um up Joe" castor and oil bait and left him the jar of scent. Also, I showed him how to reset the trap if it got sprung without a catch. That probably wasn't legal but, "Statute of Limitations"…

Over the next several weeks we took turns tearing holes in the dam and checking the trap. Sometimes the dam would be rebuilt and no activity at the trap. Or, we would find willow branches stuffed into the trap and having sprung it without any beaver. We moved the trap several times and tried several tricks to get the darned beaver to come in for a look. I would peel bark off willow branches to make it look like beaver cuttings piled up in the tap.

We were just about frustrated as Hell and ready to sit out there at night with shotguns to try a new approach. I decided we should give it one more night. We moved the trap a little closer to the dam, put all new cuttings in it, and baited it with a new batch of scent.

The next morning, I had a call - "we got 'im". I met my pal at the dam and saw the large beaver in the live trap. It appeared he had fought hard to escape. We decided to drag the trap up to the trail, put it in the truck, and made a plan for where to take it for release. It had taken a lot of effort and time to catch this danged thing and we were just about ready to just shoot him. When we got to the trap, I noticed the beaver had broken his middle finger trying to fight his way out. It sorta stuck out in an awkward way, as if the beaver was trying to tell me something! I guess Ol' Bucky Beaver got the last word on this caper.

# Chapter 18 - "Cascade Field & Stream Club"

I transferred to the Cle Elum Fish and Wildlife enforcement station in August 1985. The Officer transferring out stayed around a few days to help me get acclimated and introduced me to a few people. He suggested I attend a meeting of the Field & Stream Club to meet some of the local sportsmen.

I went to the next meeting of the Cascade Field & Stream Club out on Bullfrog Road and introduced myself. The first thing I learned was that the club president was upset with the Department for, in his words, "killing off all the elk in the Teanaway"!! I offered to answer questions and to help the club if I could. But that's another story.

The club had formed in 1934 when the State Game Department took over management of the State's wildlife resources. Previously the Counties managed all hunting and fishing. They had a nice little clubhouse, very rustic, with a wood stove for heat. There was a 300-yard rifle range and two trap houses. The range was situated near the town of Roslyn but almost every man in the Upper County was a member and no one complained of noise. The property was leased from the Burlington Northern Company (later Plum Creek Timber Co) for $1 a year.

In the interest of public relations, I decided to join the club as a regular member. In 1985 the annual dues were $10. I got to know some of the members and volunteered for projects such as work parties. I found that the club sponsored hunter education classes taught by members. I began helping with that effort and taught the wildlife enforcement section every year. The club also put on an annual kid's fishing derby at the old Bullfrog Ponds. There were fun shoots on the range where winners went home with a pound of bacon or a turkey.

One year we had some new people voted in with some more progressive ideas. The annual Bullfrog Mountain Man Rendezvous was started, and we decided to put on a fundraiser banquet. We started a life membership drive to raise more funds to purchase the property from Plum Creek. To get things going I purchased the first Life Membership for $500.

Then the hammer fell! Plum Creek announced they were selling the entire 7,000-acre Bullfrog tree farm to a resort developer. *Horrified* was the word of the day! We tried to work with the new landowner to see if a shooting range would work into their plans, where resort goers could come target shooting.

In 1999 we were told that the club would have to move, and the gate was closed for good. This was devastating to the members. Thinking that was the end of it most members drifted away, leaving a small group of us to decide what to do with the club. We had raised quite a bit of money, so we started looking around for a place to move our range.

After a great deal of effort and help from some members who were involved in real estate, we found a piece of land on Hayward Hill, 184 acres on a hilltop half way between Cle Elum and

Ellensburg. Aside from the wind, it was ideal, and it had lots of room to develop a great shooting range. The landscape was covered in Bitterbrush and Sagebrush and provided terrific deer and elk habitat. With the help of a cash donation from the resort company we were able to purchase the land outright in 2001. And, speaking of wind, a wind power company had moved into the area on the hill and approached us regarding putting a couple of towers on our land. Did I mention the wind?

Then reality set in. The land had been cattle pasture and was not zoned for a shooting range. We had to apply for a zone change, to "Forest and Range". This took time but was finally approved by the county. Then we needed a conditional use permit. The first attempt failed and there was huge opposition from neighboring property owners. The nearest home was over a mile away, but opponents feared loud noise and bullets zinging all over the area.

In 2001, with the help of a land attorney and several club members involved in land management, we were granted a CUP to develop a shooting range on our land. At a public hearing many of us spoke to the need for a range in the county. Also, there was a need for a police training range as all local law enforcement traveled out of county for their firearms training. I spoke with several members of the opposition and promised our intent to follow all the noise and safety conditions laid out in the Permit.

With several grants and many, many volunteers from the membership, we were able to build a great facility. We had a rifle range that included some steel gongs out to 400 yards, a 35-yard pistol range, Archery targets from 10 to 60 yards, and a road down to an area we hoped to have developed for local law enforcement. We also had a large pole building which, when finally enclosed, would be used for storage and meetings.

I was extremely proud to have been involved with this effort. I was the Vice President for several years and my wife had become the Secretary. Our group was like a well-oiled machine and we had mostly built the place by hand, from a dirt pile to a first-class shooting range. We developed a website and before we knew it our membership had grown to 700 members from all over the state. We decided to cap the membership to control the growth.

After a large range fire (The Taylor Bridge Fire) blew through our property we joined a class-action lawsuit against the construction outfit that caused the fire. With a whole lot of effort from our Secretary, we successfully got over $67,000 in compensation. With that we were able to rebuild our perimeter fences and have the property reseeded with native grasses. I organized an effort with the Mule Deer Foundation to replant Bitterbrush plugs and seed on the sloped area away from the shooting ranges. We got 30 volunteers to spend a whole day planting.

After being a member of the club for over 36 years I feel very satisfied with the facility we ended up with. There are plans to build a trap/skeet range, improve the law enforcement range, and double the size of the pistol range. It just seems to get better every day. We have a great relationship with the wind farm company, and, in fact, their manager is now our Vice President. He and his whole crew are members. (Google cascadefieldandstream.com).

**Eight shooting benches in the rifle shed**

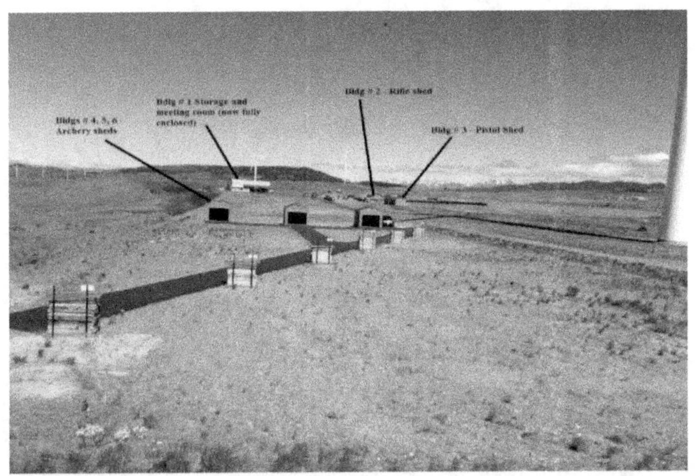


**The Cascade Field & Stream Club in 2020 - note the windmills to the right and in the distance.**

# Chapter 19 - "Problem Elk"

**Photo by Bob Bailey**

Over the course of 35 years, I was heavily involved in elk management, elk damage resolution, elk herding, and elk hunting. Right out of Colorado State University in 1977 I was hired for a summer job at the prestigious Vermejo Park Ranch near Raton, New Mexico. Working with the Ranch Wildlife Manager, Dr. Gary Wolfe (future President and CEO of The Rocky Mountain Elk Foundation), I was fortunate to learn about general population management and harvest data as well as disease control. The ranch had over 6000 elk on its 500,000+ acres and hunters paid a fair chunk of change for the privilege to vie for a trophy bull.

After that summer and staying on as a hunting guide through the end of December, I had a wealth of experience with elk. When I was hired by the Washington Game Department as a control agent I got to use that experience by knocking my head against a wall trying to keep elk out of hay fields. After many years I came to the realization that you can herd elk anywhere they want to go and hardly ever where *I* wanted them to go.

**Herding elk from one hay field to another**

I was hand-picked to transfer to the Cle Elum area based mainly on my vast experience in elk control. And, boy, did I need it. My first season, during the 2nd cutting of hay, I got to know a whole bunch of landowners very well. If I recall, there were at least 29 different hay farmers calling me to complain about herds of elk in their fields. Then, after the hay was all cut and put in barns, the calls were about getting elk out of the barns. There was no way I could be in more than one place at a time, so I started handing out Cracker shells, 12-gauge M-80 shells, like they were candy and asking the landowners to please try to help me out. Truth be known, I think most of those Cracker shells were horded and used on the 4th of July and New Year's Eve.

People are all different, even hay farmers. Some are passionately irate about the elk while others are very nice and helpful. I had folks calling to tell me they were going to start shooting if I didn't get "my" G**D***ed elk out of there. I knew one old guy that usually apologized for bothering me with his problem elk. Many were understanding while demanding relief at the same time. Much of the Timothy Hay in Kittitas County is exported to Japan and is worth more dollars per ton than I was getting paid per month. I always meant to talk with someone in the Olympia payroll office about that!

I never knew why but it seemed the elk liked to be in areas with high concentrations of mosquitos. The elk had learned to come out at night due to all the harassment during the daylight hours. I would go out just before dark to one field or another and sit in the brush waiting. That was the best time of day to find hungry mosquitos. I don't know if the elk could smell the repellent I had on or if they saw me swatting at the bugs, but they seemed to hold off coming out to the fields until I finally gave up and went home. Then I would get that irate call to come back out.

I had some farm fields that were adjacent to the irrigation canal. The elk would come out of the woods, swim the canal, and chow down in the hay field all night. I used to sit on that canal bank, swatting mosquitos, until the elk started crossing and then shoot Cracker shells to scare them back to the woods. It was fun to see their eyes bug out from fright. But, as soon as I left, thinking I had outsmarted them, they would come back across to eat *their* dinner. How'd they know?

We had several Zonn Guns, machines that ran on propane and ignited every so often with a loud boom. I would place these out in hay fields and set them to go off at night, all night, every ten minutes. The only thing they bothered were nearby people trying to sleep. I've seen photos of elk laying near the guns chewing their cuds and not moving when they boomed.

Sometimes I would ask the landowners if they would let hunters come in and put some pressure on the elk. We even started a special "damage control hunt" area that encompassed many of the hay farms in the county. Lots of elk were harvested and it actually was making a difference. Some farmers would take their tractors out and lift the dead elk so the hunters could field dress them and load them in trucks.  Eventually the Master Hunter Program was used to get highly trained, experienced and ethical sportsmen on to farms near homes and towns to help.

One particular rancher who complained often and loudly to me eventually became a good friend. I remember one day he was yelling at me about the elk knocking down his fences. I responded by telling him his fences were dying of old age and he should consider rebuilding them. Oh, that helped a lot! At one point we agreed to never say the three-letter word "elk" to each other because he would get so worked up. Finally, when we had a damage control season for cow elk, he asked me if I would like to hunt on his two and a half sections of land. I was floored, but of course I accepted. He said it was mainly because I knew every inch of his ranch and he felt I could probably kill one of those damned three letter words. When I took a cow, I offered him some of the meat. That sealed the deal, and we became friends. I was fortunate to harvest 6 cows on the ranch. And he let me guide other "good" hunters that I could vouch for. He has since passed away and I miss visiting with him about things like golf, or the Seahawks, or….anything but elk.

H25
WR 83
SUSPECT ELK

# Chapter 20 - "Public Relations"

Most game wardens, especially those in rural counties, know very well that they have to live in the area with many of the people they interact with. "Tread lightly but carry a big stick". One thing I learned right away was that a lot of Kittitas County folks were related, and I put my foot in my mouth several times while discussing my enforcement activities with people. "Hey, Fred Smith is my cousin, Jackass!"

Public relations are a huge part of our job. If people didn't trust or respect you, they could have a very negative effect on life. I decided right from the start that I needed to get in good with the locals, at least some of them. I also knew you can't please everyone.

So, I joined the Field & Stream Club and got to know a whole bunch of what I called "my hunting public". I developed a good relationship with the local weekly paper - not an easy feat as many a story can get edited and misinterpreted, and people could get the wrong idea. That's why many LE Officers don't trust reporters (or lawyers). I started submitting articles about local wildlife events, information on hunting and fishing rules, and the occasional war story (minus any names, of course) or request for help or information on an investigation. Every year I would write up something about bears ("don't feed them your garbage or bird feeders").  Eventually a new reporter showed up in town and he promised to always tell my information straight. We became trusted friends and I even have his direct phone line for good scoops.

One of my great ambitions was teaching Hunter Education classes to young, new hunters. I thought, if we could get the right information to them, stress ethics and sportsmanship, we could keep them from learning bad hunting practices from "Uncle Joe" or "Grandpa Fred". I accepted many requests to speak to school kids and helped out with some 5th grade outdoors programs.

Working and having coffee with other Officers from different local agencies made a huge difference for me if I ever needed backup. Most of the Deputies and Troopers would come running to help me because they knew I would always do the same for them. Especially in a rural area where there is not a lot of backup nearby. I was almost always alone.

I've worked closely with our local Department of Transportation on places to put deer/elk crossing signs and was allowed to use their "dump" pit for road kills or unusable seized animals.

I got to know our local wildlife rehabilitation operators, especially a veterinarian in Ellensburg who would always take injured critters I brought in. I took in an injured bald eagle found on a farm north of town. It was diagnosed with lead poisoning. After a month of rehab, it was healthy enough to release. I contacted the local newspaper and radio station, as well as the grade school, about the release date and time at the farm. We ended up with a large crowd of onlookers as the healthy eagle flew off toward the hills

**Preparing to release rehabbed bald eagle.**

For several years our Field & Stream Club entered a group in the annual Pioneer Days Parade on 4th of July weekend. We had an antique fire engine that some members would ride on and a bunch of us would walk the route in mountain man clothing and shooting off muzzleloaders filled with paper. We sure made a racket and had a lot of fun. One year I put our elk decoy in the back of my patrol truck with some pine branches and called it a parade float. It was a hit but there were a lot of folks taking aim with imaginary rifles. I yelled "verbal warnings" at them from my window.

I would like to pass on a very important PR tip to other law enforcement officers - don't write your local Sheriff a ticket, like I did!! I was checking some of our river access areas one winter day and found 17 vehicles parked at the Thorp Access on the Yakima River. Not a one had a Vehicle Access Permit displayed as required. My first thought was, "Yes! 17 easy tickets and I'm outta here". Hoping to get the job done before these people arrived from their boating trip on the river and get into a big screamer, I decided to hold off running all the license plates through the system. All I needed on the Notice of Infraction (a minor, non-criminal ticket) was the charge and amount, the vehicle license, and to write "Registered Owner" in the name space. Then I placed the violator copy on the windshield. I was in and gone before anyone arrived. A couple hours later I decided to finish my paperwork. I parked and ran the plates on my laptop. I figured this was a group of Yuppies that do this every winter. They float the river and sip wine, calling it fun as they freeze their tails off. As I ran the plates for owner information, I found one came back to our Kittitas County Sheriff. Oh, oh! I've known this guy for many years, call him a friend, and never knew he was one of those wine sipping yuppies. Sheesh. Now what do I do - I already left a ticket on his windshield! Well, it was too late to do anything this day and I went home.

The following morning, dragging my feet all the way, I went to the Sheriff's home and knocked on the door. His wife answered the door and I very sheepishly asked to see the Sheriff. I was hanging my head when he came to the door. It seems he had a whole house full of family. He said, "well hi Steve, how's things". I explained that I didn't know it was his car at the access and I was sorry about the ticket. He told me not to worry, that he knew they were wrong parking there, and that I had done the right thing. Whew! Later, I found out he had actually gone into court, asked the judge for leniency, and paid $25 for his violation. And he went and bought a Vehicle Access Permit. We still speak to this day, but not about the ticket.

Back when I started in Tacoma I was told to write up a report of all of my public relations contacts for the year '84-'85. It was fairly easy to go back through my daily notebook and find the information my boss wanted. Looking back over that list was an eye opener - I seemed to be so busy with PR that there wasn't much time for my day job.

I took lots of "riders" along on my travels - various sportsmen, law enforcement officers from different agencies, reporters. I did interviews with news people who usually misquoted me but made an effort to get the story out about my job as a Control Agent - I always stressed that people should not leave their pet food out for the raccoons and bears. There were Hunter Education classes at the Tacoma Sportsmen's Association, Trapper Ed. classes, presentations at school career days, monthly breakfast meetings with other law enforcement groups, and various public meetings. I met regularly with the Trapper's Association to discuss trapping seasons and regulations, animal complaints, and recommendations for regulation changes to present to the Game Commission.

Steve Rogers turned his Game Department pickup truck off the road near Spanaway Creek, climbed from the cab and pulled a pair of hipboots onto his feet and legs.

Taking a long-handled cultivator from the bed of the truck, Rogers climbed through a fence at the edge of the road and set off across a meadow through which the creek wound toward some trees on the other side.

Rogers is a wildlife-control agent, one of about 10 who work for the Game Department, and his purpose there that morning was to break up a beaver dam that had been flooding a man's horse pasture along the creek.

He stepped into the water, and

Sometimes, though, they eventually give up, and move on to find a friendlier neighborhood.

Rogers walked back to his truck and headed for a second location in southern Pierce County, this time to place a live trap on a tiny creek in an effort to corral another flood-causing beaver.

He prefers to live-trap problem animals, he said, and was tearing down parts of some dams this day only because some of his traps were being repaired.

"Just recently nearly my whole job has been beaver control," he said. "The trappers didn't take many last season, because they thought the prices would be down. And now I've got 'em coming out of my ears."

When Rogers catches

**Tacoma News Tribune article by Bob Mottram, 1982**

I hauled trout to the Boy Scout Scout-O-Rama at McCord Air Force Base and pheasants to various release sites in nearby counties. I got to help the Fish Biologists with electro-fishing at local lakes and streams, and then explained the program to local fishermen and residents. Several of us met with Komo 4 News after we captured two cougars and released them with radio collars. More TV interviews involved my job, urban problem wildlife, and once up the White River area after one of our Officers, Terry Hoffer, was shot and killed by a hunter - I was on TV with that one. I got involved with a local Boy Scout Troop, became Assistant Scout Master, and helped the kids with merit badges on Nature, Fish & Wildlife Management, Botany, Mammals, and public speaking. The Scoutmaster was a WSP Trooper friend, and we had several years of great experiences out on hikes and campouts, passing on our knowledge to the kids. Luckily no kids ever got hurt playing with knives, axes, and fires.

After moving to Cle Elum an awful lot of my "PR" time consisted of appeasing farmers with elk problems. It took great effort to work with them and get them to help me with "their" problems. I won't call myself a "silver-tongued devil" but I did manage to get some of those folks to shoot cracker shells at the elk instead of .30-06 bullets. And I did work very hard to get them financial compensation for their crop damage.

I never thought I got paid enough for all the great PR I did for this department, but it was fulfilling and helped me in getting along with my public.

# Chapter 21 - "What the Hell am I doing here?"

Back in '85, when I was transferring to the Cle Elum duty station, I had heard lots of stories about my new Pardner - wild rumors about what a tough guy he was, a pool player, drinker, fighter, who would arrest his own mother. Here I was a "beaver trapper" from Tacoma moving over to work with this famous law man. Needless to say I was a little nervous and intimidated.

When I moved to Cle Elum this "Mad Man" showed up with a whole gang of helpers. We drank a bunch of beer before we got done moving in. Hmm, I thought, this ain't so bad. That was my first impression.

Two days later, before I was "officially" on duty here, he called and needed me to help with a fire on the LT Murray Wildlife Area south of Ellensburg. Three days later, after he tried to kill me by backing me into the fire-line on the pumper truck and having to jump over rattlesnakes in the dark, I came dragging home tired, hungry, and wondering, "What the Hell am I doing here?"

That same fall, my first elk season working the Colockum Wildlife Area, there was a huge shootout up in the Parke Creek area. Several extra cow elk were left laying after the smoke cleared. I was assigned to help field dress the elk for salvage by the food bank. The first thing I did was run a very sharp knife into my knee. A Deputy said it looked like I was going into shock - he carried me to his vehicle and drove me to the ER. After stitches and a couple days off I was really wondering, "What the Hell am I doing here?"

My Pard, Wild Bill, said I needed a horse for back country patrol. He found me a great deal on a registered Quarter Horse mare, 3 years old and green broke. Ok, I thought, not knowing what "Green Broke" meant. Her name was Cookie. Well, we tried to load this mare into our little two-horse trailer, and she reared up, getting her front feet stuck up on the manger. Hmmm. Not a good start to my horsemanship career.


So, the first time I rode her she threw me about twenty feet in the air and ran off. "Okay", I growled! After that we kinda reached an understanding - I'm in charge and you do what I want you to do! Wild Bill told me to make sure she knows who the boss is. She never did figure that out, but we sure covered a lot of miles over 20 years.

That summer we took a horse patrol, into the Wilderness above Lake Cle Elum, to check the High Lakes.  We camped along the Pacific Crest Trail just below Deep Lake, about 13 miles in from the trailhead. Bill brought his good Buckskin ropin' horse and I rode my Cookie mare. It was just a beautiful night in the High Lonesome.

That ropin' horse started snorting about 2 am and fell over dead, astraddle the Crest Trail. Well, it was a sorry situation. We had to quarter Ol' Buck up into pieces to pack him away from the trail so it wouldn't attract bears where all the granola crunchers hike. We threw our gear on my horse and hiked out of there. During that whole trip out on foot I was thinking, "What the Hell am I doing here?"

After getting all those kinks out the first year, we had a great time for the next 18 years, kicking bad guy butt, chasing elk, fixing elk fence after chasing them through it, and working horse patrols for hunting and fishing seasons. Finally, one day, Ol' Bill said he was gonna hang up his spurs and retire. We had worked with a lot of great guys over the years, had lots of memories, and now I was going to be the only game warden in the county. Someone called me the Lone Ranger. I said, "that's Lone Rogers to you". It was just coming on hunting season when we had his retirement party, and I was getting calls from ranchers about elk in their hay fields. It kinda got me thinking, "What the Hell am I doing here?"

Well, we got the Sarge retired, and he and the wife went off pronghorn hunting in Wyoming. I got a great new Sergeant and another Officer to help. So, what the Hell, I'm here and making the best of things. That's what the Hell I'm doing here.

**Wild Bill Essman, Sgt., wife Deborah, and Rogers tellin' lies**

# Chapter 22 - "Don't fight over elk"

During an early muzzleloader elk season, I was called to the scene of a dispute over a big 6-point bull elk, a real beauty. Two guys were arguing over who actually killed the elk. After much discussion and negotiating it was agreed by all parties that they would split the elk - One guy took the meat and the other the antlers. To keep things legal, I made them both notch their elk tags, and I wrote a note to each regarding the split. End of story and all happy campers. That's what I thought.

Later that fall, during the *late* muzzleloader elk season, I heard the Sheriff's Office put out a report of a missing elk hunter in the Teanaway Valley. (It was also the same area as the previous situation above). The overdue hunter was one of a large group that hunt there every year and he was well able to take care of himself in the hills, often staying out overnight to trail an elk. But his friends and family were worried about him.

I arrived and offered to help with the search. The family knew approximately where the guy would be hunting and we set off in the dark, on snowshoes, to look for sign. Somewhere around 8 pm I heard radio talk that the subject's body had been found. The Sheriff, now on scene, asked if I would take my 35mm camera and document the situation. The coroner had been summoned. When several Deputies and I got to the location of the body we assumed the subject had died of a heart attack. He was lying face down in the snow and a wad of gum was frozen to his lips. His muzzleloader rifle was lying next to him.

I took a bunch of photos prior to anyone moving the body. When we rolled him over we could see a wound on his belly area. Also, when we rolled him over I recognized him as one of the two fighting over the elk in the early season. It turned out he had been stabbed. We searched the area for a knife, to no avail. The Sheriff decided this was a crime scene and we all backed off, waiting for the coroner.

It was very cold out there in the dark and snow. We decided to start a warming fire and stood around it while waiting for the coroner to arrive. During the conversation I mentioned this was one of the subjects in an earlier dispute over an elk. Nobody else knew about it or had any idea who the other guy in the dispute was.

Later I discussed this with a Detective and retrieved the information from my notebook regarding the dispute in the earlier season. I had all the needed information and it led to the arrest of the other guy. He was charged with 2nd Degree Murder.

The suspect was cooperative and turned over the knife he had used. His story was that the two of them had been hunting the late season and met each other on a ridge in the forest. He said an argument ensued over the early season incident and the other, much bigger guy got violent and attacked him. He said he was scared and was able to get his knife out to defend himself. As the bigger guy grabbed him he thrust his knife into his gut. That stopped the fight. He got scared and left for his cabin.

My burning question was, "why were they even out hunting again after they had both notched their elk tags in the early season?". And, how in the world did they happen to bump into each other again in all of that big country?

The guy that was killed was buried and the knifer was found guilty of a lesser charge of Manslaughter after the jury heard his side of the story.

I was involved in many disputes over deer and elk during my career and they were nearly always resolved with no hard feelings. There were a few times when it was impossible to reach an agreement and I would take the animal for donation to the food bank. But it was very unusual to end up in a murder investigation over a stinkin' elk. What the…..?!

# Chapter 23 - "Ol' No Name, Game Warden"

As narrated by Festus Hagen of Gunsmoke fame:

Well, Ol' No Name weren't no racehorse and he sure weren't much to look at. But you could tell lookin' in his eyes he was special – a kind horse with a big heart, and always willin' to do the job. That job, for about 25 years of his life, was packin' Game Wardens around in the hills chasin' bad guys and campin' out in the beautiful wilderness areas of Kittitas County.

Why "No Name"? Wail it just sorta fit him. No one really knew what breed he was, kinda like a Heinz 57 sort of feller. We tried namin' him Lightening but it never took. He just weren't lightening material. My ol' partner, Frank Cram, tried to name him Blaze. We all agreed Blaze was a nice name, but it just didn't suit him. When we was up in the hills I always called him "Big Guy", just between the two of us. Ifn anyone else was around it was Ol' No Name for sure. I called him "Pokey" a few times when I was ridin' the mare and leadin' Ol' No Name up the trail. She was perty quick and he just weren't in no hurry, pert-near tore my arm outta the socket draggin' him along.

The Old Game Department bought Ol' No Name from an outfitter up in Okanogan, way back around 1980 or so. He was just 7 years old then and, I'm told, a fair looking young gelding with lots of muscle and a bit of an attitude in his eyes. He was placed into service by the Game Wardens in Kittitas and Chelan Counties and made lots of trips to the wilderness. His size made him an excellent packer and he was an easy rider, too, his big feet never missin' a step ('cept when a danged ol' elk ran across the trail ahead of him).

Somewhere in the next couple of years he got a little too much spring grass and he foundered. He came out of it perty okay but he had some pain and swelling in his neck which never went away. Sometimes I wondered ifn he wasn't playin' it up to get sympathy. He looked perty sad with is head ahangin' just ofn the ground.

The backpackers on the trail always liked Ol' No Name and some of them offered him their Gorp. I always told them he really likes that Gorp stuff. For them backpackers who didn't offer their Gorp I always told 'em to git way back off the trail 'cause this ol' horse is a mean one and likes to kick! You shoulda saw 'em scamper off the trail to git outta his way. It were great folly.

I met ol' No Name back in '85 when I transferred to the Cle Elum District as the "new" Game Warden. Hell, ever one thought I was a new guy, but I'd already had six years on and I felt like an old veteran.

My ol' Boss and I made plenty of trips to the high country to check fishermen and hunters. Sometimes we'd pack Ol' No Name, sometimes we'd ride him. Heck, he didn't mind either way, jest as long as he got to go. Ted Ford was ridin' Ol' No Name headin' in to Waptus Lake one year to help me work the High Hunt. We run into the ugliest batch of misfits, Llamas and goats, all packed up like a string of mules an' bein' lead by some Hippie, long-haired dudes from Seattle. When Ol' No Name seen them he musta thought, "that ain't no mule string, it's the pack string from Hell!" What happened next was not perty but I must say I was real proud of Ol' No Name and Ted – No Name made a pure half gainer in mid-air, swappin' ends so fast, and Ted hangin' on for dear life, legs aflyin' around, and 'bout had the saddle horn tore off.  Last, I seen 'em they was both a-spittin' and a-gittin' down the trail to the trailer. But that's another story.

My wife, Cindy, had the privilege, or honor, or somethin' like thet, of being Ol' No Name's personal trainer. She was always impressed 'bout how smart he was. Like, he always knew when to stop ifn there was a juicy bit of grass alongside the trail when we was out gitten the critters legged up for a trip to the hills. Funny how he was so smart he gained weight whilst exercisin'.

And Ol' No Name was too smart to get his feet all wet and muddy by walkin' through a crick (he was very environmental minded). Why, he'd gather hisself up and launch his huge bulk all the way across the wet area and land clear on the other side without touchin' any of that mud. I could see how Cindy really enjoyed jumpin' over cricks like that 'cause her eyes was wide open and she had a big ol' grin on her face. 'leastwise it looked like a grin. Musta been perty thrillin' for her.

The best trick she ever taught Ol' No Name was to load up in the trailer all by hisself. Why, she'd jest open the door, toss the lead rope over his back, and he'd hop in. She's say, "wow, he sure is a smart horse". I guess he was at that 'cause after all his years he's learnt that when he got them greenhorns ofn his back he could go for a nice ride home and git fed and spoilt.

Well, Ol' No Name turned 30, or 28 or so, back in '03, and after years of hard work, he was gittin' a little tired. He kinda whispert to me one day, something about havin' enough. I'd noticed that last fall, comin' outta the hi hunt up by Pollalie Ridge, he were walkin' kinda slow. His foot Doc, Mr. Simmons, the shoer, said he thought the old guy was gittin' kinda stiff in the joints. I decided it was time to retire him and let him git some rest.

I talked around and finally got ahold of the folks at the Dragonwood Ranch on Lookout Mountain. They's got a heart of gold and fell in love with Ol' No Name. They agreed to adopt the poor ol' guy and let him live out his life in luxury at their place. I ain't never seed a horse git such good treatment and git so spoilt. He got fed special senior diet cakes. Ifn his neck looked like it hurt he got a chiropractor to massage him. He even has his own stall and exercise area, and in the summer he had the run of the whole ranch. I tell ya, he's worked this retirement gig into quite a scam.

Seems there was this ol' mare in the next stall and she an' Ol' No Name kinda took a shine to each other. She had been named "Gramma" by the folks at Dragonwood. You know, it didn't take long for them to name Ol' No Name "Gramps". One day, when I stopped to check on Ol' No Name, they said, "Gramps is over there by the pasture watching over the new foals". I said, "Gramps!?" Well, By Golly, after all these years Ol' No Name finally got him a real name. It's now the summer of 2006 and Ol' Gramps is still kickin' up at Dragonwood. I figure the way he's milkin' this new gig he may stick around another ten years or so. After all, he's barely had time to git acquainted with his new handle.

OL' NO NAME
STILL KICKIN' 01/2010 — AGE 40

# Chapter 24 - "Who am I working for anyway?"

Way back in the dark ages of the 1970s and '80s I was hired by the Washington State Department of Game. Ah, those were the good old days, and the entire department was like a big family. Everybody, including hatchery and game farm managers, biologists, and a few others could do enforcement work and write tickets. It was especially helpful to have all that extra help during hunting seasons, like working check stations.

At some point someone got the idea that we managed not only game animals but all wildlife of the state. That's when our name got changed to the Department of Wildlife. Yep, that was expensive - new badges, new patches, logos, letterhead, etc. I guess it made sense but, for some of us who had been around a little while, it was a difficult transition. At about that same time my supervisory chain of command changed from the regional biologist to the regional enforcement agent. We beaver trappers were trained and issued firearms (S&W Model 66 revolvers in .357 Mag.), different patches again, and were expected to work enforcement when we had some downtime in the wildlife control business.

Also, around this time, it was decided to stop giving enforcement commissions to non-enforcement people. This was due to increased training and liability. It was yet another change to how the entire system worked and caused many people who used to write tickets to be upset about it. It didn't help that Enforcement got a pay raise due to the increased training and duties.

In July 1994, 9 years after I had transferred to the enforcement station in Cle Elum, we had another, much more encompassing change. Someone with a lot more wisdom than most of us mere employees decided that the Dept. of Fisheries and Dept. of Wildlife should merge and become the Dept. of Fish & Wildlife. It may have made sense to some but most of us wildlife folks didn't want "them fish cops" in our ranks. And, the fish cops felt the same about us. Merger was not an easy transition. But, after a lot of cross-training and time, we did merge.

**Merger of Fisheries and Wildlife**

The former Department of Fisheries was tasked with managing the food fish (salmon, shellfish, etc.) resources of the state and Wildlife managed game fish and wildlife species (trout and other game fish, game and non-game animals). There was some intense training and lots of meetings and after some time we found that many of the fish cops were pretty ok people. I had worked with a couple of the Fisheries guys on river habitat/hydraulics projects and learned they liked to hunt and fish and go to the mountains.

By the time I retired in 2011 we had several reformed fish cops working in Eastern Washington wildlife enforcement stations and they seemed to be getting along fine. I guess it really was for the best for the resources in the long run. And I doubt there will be any more major changes in the big scheme of things. There have been some changes, like going back to having wildlife control specialists instead of the enforcement guys doing it all. The Enforcement Division went through some heavy training through the Criminal Justice Training Commission, gained State and National accreditation, and finally we were granted full police powers in Washington. After many, many changes over 33 years I finally knew who I was working for.

STATE GAME CONTROL
STATE OF WASHINGTON
DEPARTMENT OF GAME
WILDLIFE ENFORCEMENT
WASHINGTON
DEPARTMENT OF WILDLIFE
WILDLIFE ENFORCEMENT
WASHINGTON
GAME DEPARTMENT
ENFORCEMENT
WASHINGTON
DEPARTMENT OF
FISH AND WILDLIFE

# Chapter 25 - "Spike-Only elk season"

Washington State has had great elk hunting opportunities for many years. There are several main herds across the State including the Colockum and Yakima herds on the Eastern slopes of the Cascade Mountains. Since before I was hired the elk have been heavily hunted and were thriving. There were so many elk that they started generating complaints by ranchers. Elk were tearing down fences, trampling pastures, and eating tons of expensive export-grade Timothy hay. Seasons were open for any bull elk and many areas had drawings for antlerless (cow) elk permits, all in an effort to keep the elk in check.

Big game biologists started noticing fewer adult bulls and younger, inferior bulls breeding cows. This was causing some cows to be bred late and calf survival was down. Other states were seeing similar problems and were testing the idea of a spike-only season to allow branch-antlered bulls to advance to adult breeding age. Washington jumped on board with that idea in the mid-1990s and there was a huge outcry from the elk hunting public.

We enforcement guys were worried there would be problems with hunters shooting branch-antlered bulls either out of ignorance or in spite of the new rules. We anticipated problems and asked for Fish & Wildlife Officers from around the state to come assist us during elk seasons in Kittitas and Yakima Counties. That first spike-only elk season in 1994 was definitely one to remember.

A spike antlered bull elk was defined as any male elk with a clean, unbranched antler on one side. The other side could have any number of points. As long as it had a spike on one side it was legal to harvest. I hate to say it, but we had a lot of branch-antlered bulls killed that first season. Many were left to rot when hunters realized it was a spike-only season.

Two of us were sitting along Manastash Road south of Ellensburg on opening morning watching with spotting scopes as a herd of elk was moving along the ridge a half mile above the road. It seemed like there were hunters and looky-loos everywhere, all watching these elk. We could see several hunters on the ridge wearing hunter orange clothes, in pursuit of the herd. There was about 5 inches of snow on the ground.

I saw a 5x5 (5 points on each side) bull in the group as he walked along the side hill. Suddenly there was a shot and I saw the 5-point bull go down. We could see two people near the elk and more shots erupted. I guess they thought it wasn't dead yet. It is very seldom we get to actually witness a violation in progress, but this was definitely not a spike bull being shot.

One of the two hunters started walking away toward a road on the ridge.  I had my partner take off to meet the guy at the road while I continued to keep an eye on the elk. The Officer made contact with the hunter as he arrived at his vehicle. He said he was hurrying to get more ammo. What did he need more ammo for? Well, he had been "trying to shoot the branched antlers off to make it a spike". That direct quote went into the case report when the guy was issued a mandatory court appearance summons for killing a branched bull during the closed season (only open for spikes).

The rest of the day, in fact the rest of the 9-day season, we were running all over the county on reports of illegal kills. Most of the reports were from honest hunters turning in others for shooting branched bulls. If someone reports a poaching incident, and we can make a case (charge the violator), the reporting party may be eligible for points toward a special permit drawing. This first season there were a lot of points given and, in some cases, the reporting parties were turning in their own hunting friends. Heck, ten points toward a branched bull permit was worth it. Cell phones are wonderful things.

We had an arrangement with the Union Gospel Mission in Yakima to pick up any animals that were salvageable and could be given out to needy people. I lost track of how many trips they made up to Ellensburg to meet us to pick up multiple seized elk.

By the last day of that modern firearm elk season, with heavy snows and heavy hunting pressure, hundreds of elk had been pushed down toward the lowlands and hay farms. There were still hunters desperately trying to fill their tags. This turned out to be a bad combination. A herd of about 200 elk had been pushed down to an area near Elk Heights just off I-90 and were trapped above the elk fence that ran parallel to the freeway. This property was private and just below the LT Murray Wildlife Area.

**Two branch-antlered bulls**

A group of hunters who had permission to hunt this private land were in place and took a shot at a spike bull. Then, there were other hunters in the area who must have thought it was okay to hunt here and started shooting.

I was about 5 miles away in the Taneum Creek area when I got a call from a neighboring landowner at Elk Heights. He was irate and demanding immediate response because, "all Hell is breaking loose". I called for additional help on the radio and started toward Elk Heights.

By the time I got there the dust was just starting to settle. From the main road just off the freeway exit I could see Orange-clad hunters out in the fields and several elk lying in the snow. The herd had been chased off to the west and I could hear shooting in that direction. It was like an old west shootout!

I called the owner of this property and asked him to come to the scene. I had three Game Wardens, two County Deputies, and two State Troopers show up to help. When we got done, we ended up with 1 legal spike bull taken by hunters with permission, 2 spikes and a 6x6 taken by Trespassers (no suspect on the 6 point bull was determined), and three dead cows that nobody wanted to claim. The Deputies handled the Trespassing arrests, and the Game Wardens took the Closed Season elk charges. The Union Gospel Mission was summoned for the six illegally taken elk. The once beautiful, snow covered prairie was now covered with blood, boot and elk tracks, and drag marks. It was a heck of an ending to a heck of a season that I will never forget. I was ready for a stiff drink and a good night's rest. The muzzleloader season for elk started the next morning.

# Chapter 26 - "What a Career"

**Headed for Yakima to work the WDFW booth**

**at the Sportsmen's show**

When I got out of college, I quickly realized that the days of goofing off and going to a few classes were over and it was time to find a job. My nice life of knowing what I had to do and when it was due was over. It scared the Hell out of me. I was no stranger to working as I had had many jobs all through school. But, trying to get hired full time by a fish and wildlife agency was a whole 'nother prospect for me.

My folks lived outside of Olympia, Wa. and, after spending a season at Vermejo Park Ranch, I headed home to stay with them a while. I started dropping into the Game Department HQ office in Olympia hoping to meet some people that could help me get started. My first and very best contact was with Mr. Mike Thorniley. I give all the credit for starting my career to Mike.

After bugging him for a couple of months he decided to get rid of me and got me an interview for a seasonal job at the Whidbey Island Game Farm raising pheasants. I actually got hired and had a foot in the door. For young people looking for a career, my advice is to pester someone to the point that they want to get rid of you by finding you a job. Even raising pheasants or building elk fence. Take it!

Well, my seasonal job went full time for two years. I got to know lots of Department folks and got lots of tips on jobs. I kept applying and interviewing and my persistence paid off with the Control Agent job in Tacoma, working under none other than Mike Thorniley. When I finally made it to the big time as a beaver and skunk trapper, I thought it couldn't get any better - being paid to work outdoors with wild animals. Man, they gave me a truck and even paid for the gas. And insurance coverage.

Several years and many experiences later I landed the enforcement job in Cle Elum. This was IT! I had a huge patrol district in some of the most beautiful country in the State, a great crew to work with, and some of the most fantastic people in the world to live and work with (I love small town folks). I got paid to ride horses and eat steaks in the mountains, check hunters and fishers for compliance with the "the regs" and chase the heck out of the elk herds on snowmobiles. I was instantly a celebrity. People called and stopped by my house at all hours of the day and night. They asked me questions, told me stories about other locals, and even confided in me about things they had done in the "past" that they don't do any more. (If any "locals" are reading this, I *know* what you did!).

I really did fall in love with the area, the people, and the abundant wildlife and habitat. Part of the job was managing these resources and, though sometimes challenging, it all added up to a fabulous experience.

I considered myself an old-style game warden and by the time I retired the job had become something different. Not all bad, but something different. With the increased law enforcement emphasis and training the "new" kids spent way more time performing duties other than what the old game guys did. There were "expectations" that must be met (meaning ticket numbers), a lot less PR, and a lot more emphasis on enforcement action. There was a whole lot less just being out there and being seen (flying the flag, so to speak). People used to tell me they saw me sneaking down a logging road somewhere and I always felt that was a great deterrent to people considering committing a game crime.  I was always popping up somewhere. When I got to Cle Elum I had been told about a certain logger who poached a lot. One day I was lost (really) on a remote logging road above Stampede Pass and I met this guy in a crummy with his crew. He asked, "What the Hell are you doing out here and how did I get here"? I said I was just keeping an eye on him, as if I had planned it. We ended up becoming friends and I never did catch him poaching.

But, beyond any of the bad stuff, it was still the best job in the world. Being out in the woods and prairies, the mountains and valleys, the creek bottoms and ridges, or even running a drift boat down the river looking for fishing violations, this was my calling in life, and I wouldn't have had it any other way. Luckiest guy in the world. What a Career and what a blessing. But it was time to quit chasing bad guys down the riverbank and get out while "the gittin' was good".  Retirement is another blessing. But geeez, I've never been so busy in my life!

# ABOUT THE AUTHOR

Steve Rogers grew up the son of an Air Force Officer, graduated high school in Nebraska in 1967, and joined the US Navy. After four years in naval intelligence, he attended Colorado State University on the GI Bill. Steve graduated in 1977 with a B.S. in Wildlife Biology. After graduation he worked a season at Vermejo Park Ranch in Raton, helping with elk studies, patrolling the many lakes, and guiding elk hunters in the fall. He was hired with Washington Game Department in Jan. 1978 as a game farmer, moving up to wildlife damage control in Tacoma, Wa., and finally to fish and wildlife enforcement in Cle Elum, Wa. He retired in Cle Elum after 33 years.

www.ingramcontent.com/pod-product-compliance
Lightning Source LLC
Chambersburg PA
CBHW071625150726
48000CB00004B/1890